VICTORIAN
D RIES

VICTO

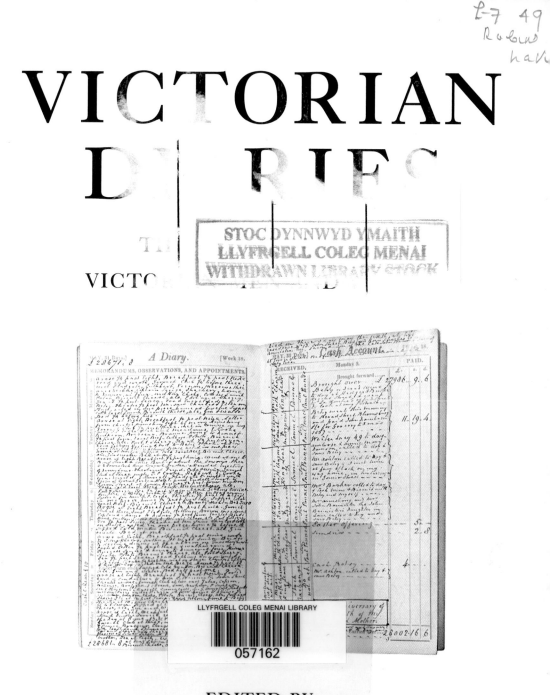

EDITED BY

HEATHER CREATON

MITCHELL BEAZLEY

SEVERAL GENERATIONS OF A VICTORIAN FAMILY POSE FOR A PHOTOGRAPH IN THEIR GARDEN

Victorian Diaries
General Editor: Heather Creaton

To Peter, again

Published in 2001 by Mitchell Beazley,
an imprint of Octopus Publishing Group Ltd
2–4 Heron Quays, London, E14 4JP

ISBN 1 84000 359 6
A CIP catalogue copy of this book is available from
the British Library.

Commissioning Editor Vivien Antwi
Executive Art Editor Kenny Grant
Project Editor Michelle Bernard
Editor Cecile Landau
Picture Research Helen Stallion, Rosie Garai
Production Nancy Roberts
Proofreader Laura Harper

Printed and bound by
Toppan Printing Company, China
Typeset in Caslon
Picture on title page: John Pritt Harley's diary
Jacket photograph: Page from a Victorian album
Note: Original spellings and punctuation in the
diary entries have been retained.

CONTENTS

INTRODUCTION

This book brings together extracts from the diaries of ordinary Victorians. Not so long ago this might have seemed a doubtful undertaking: history, like many facets of life, is subject to fashion, and for much of the last century the Victorians were regarded as deeply unfashionable. In his *Eminent Victorians* (1918) and *Queen Victoria* (1921), Lytton Strachey offered a critical reassessment of the period and its revered names, initiating a trend that was enthusiastically continued during the 1920s and 30s. The shock of War World I had brought an enormous change in social attitudes, habits and expectations, and the Victorians had come to seem stuffy and outdated. Their fashions, buildings, literature and art were commonly ridiculed, and it was not until well after World War II that a more balanced view of Victorian achievements of all kinds started to gain general respectability.

Britain was a very different place in 1901, on Queen Victoria's death at the age of 81, than it had been in 1837, when she came to the throne, aged 18. Our diary selections illustrate the diversity of Victorian life as it was really lived. One of the biggest changes was the growth in the number of Victorians: between 1841 and 1901, the UK population rose from twenty to thirty-eight million. Among the reasons for this increase were improvements in diet and standard of living, better sanitary provision and advances in medical treatment; from the 1850s onwards, many new hospitals were founded, and as a result of Florence Nightingale's reforms following the Crimean War, nurses began to be professionally trained. Infant mortality remained high throughout the period, but children who survived the first five years of life stood a good chance of living to a reasonable age. In 1837, average life expectancy was around 40 years; by 1901 it was closer to 52.

Another great change during the Victorian period was the rapid spread of industrialization. Huge factories developed, particularly in the north of England, making textiles and machinery. Mines expanded to produce the coal to fuel industry. Thousands of people were employed in mills, factories, pits and shipyards. They needed housing, so miles of countryside were swallowed up by bricks and mortar. The remaining farm land had to produce extra food for the growing population, so agriculture too had to mechanize. To help meet the increased demand, food was imported from far afield – grain from North America, frozen meat from South America and the Antipodes. Sailing ships gave way to steam; goods and passengers could be sent quickly all over the world.

Permeating all this change was a vision of the world as a place that could be improved by human organization. There was a great appetite for fact-finding and information of all kinds, typified by the enormous number of Royal Commissions set up by the government. Their detailed and analytical reports investigated a wide range of social issues including employment conditions in the mines and factories, education, sanitation, housing and other topics affecting millions of people. Numerous Acts of Parliament were passed as a result of this research, regulating these areas and many others.

Who chose the Members of Parliament responsible for passing all this legislation? The 1832 Reform Act had effectively given the right to vote to the middle classes. The Reform Acts of 1867 and 1884 extended it to the urban and agricultural working classes. Women of all classes, however, were excluded from the franchise for Parliamentary elections until well after Queen Victoria's death. Educated women resented their exclusion, and from 1867 the Women's Suffrage movement gained momentum, working for a change in the law that was not completely achieved until 1928.

Educational opportunities varied from class to class, but improved in general through the Victorian period. Upper- and middle-class boys were usually taught at home while very young, then when aged ten or so sent off to public, private or grammar schools of various kinds for the rest of their education. Girls would continue lessons with their governess, or mother, until 14 or 15, at which point some were dispatched to a ladies' boarding school to acquire a little more social polish for a year or two before 'coming out' into society. The development of academic girls' day schools from the 1850s onwards offered the chance for clever girls from liberally minded middle-class homes to get a serious education which could take them forward to the university courses that were slowly being opened up for women students.

For the working classes the options were few. State education was not provided before the 1870 Education Act, and was not compulsory even then. Depending on where they lived, working-class children might acquire a little basic education at a local charity school, at a Church of England 'National School', or at a non-denominational 'British School'. The Ragged School Union also ran schools for the poorest in some areas. The education these schools provided was necessarily fairly basic, but an impressive proportion of the population learned to read, write and do basic arithmetic, a solid background for a working life. The spread of public libraries, set up by local authorities from the 1850s, encouraged many poorer people to expand their knowledge through reading. Cheap newspapers and popular magazines also played their part in informing and amusing a wider reading public than ever before.

Information could be passed on more quickly and cheaply in other ways, too. Until 1840, people had to pay the postman for letters they received. The introduction of the penny post in that year meant that the writer of the letter paid for the stamp, leading to a huge increase in the volume of mail for business and for personal purposes. The coming of the electric telegraph was another important advance in the field of Victorian communications. By the 1850s, most large towns were connected to the system, so urgent messages could be sent down the wires to the receiving office, where they were copied down and delivered to the addressee's door. One of our diarists, Maria Cust, saw the new Atlantic telegraph cable waiting to be laid in 1857. Soon, submarine cables linked Britain to the United States and to Europe, allowing news to travel faster than ever before, and revolutionizing newspaper reporting. In the 1880s, the telephone was enthusiastically welcomed by businesses and home subscribers, and by the 1890s recording equipment was available – Andrew Tait was fascinated to hear the voice of Gladstone in this way. These rapid and revolutionary technological changes made the same sort of impact on daily life that the internet and the mobile phone were to make in the late 20th century.

Such developments built on and added to the enormous effect that the transport revolution had had on the national economy and on social life. At the beginning of Queen Victoria's reign, for example, it took several days to travel from London to Edinburgh by road or sea. By the end of her reign it was a 10-hour train journey. Railways spread rapidly all over the country, making even remote rural areas easily accessible to the traveller. The advent of the safety bicycle in the 1880s opened up the countryside for many young people who, either alone or in cycle clubs, could explore their neighbourhood on day excursions or longer tours. By the end of the Victorian age, pioneering holidaymakers were also travelling by car, though this would be an expensive and exclusive form of transport for many years to come. Foreign travel also became easier throughout the period, especially with the availability of organized package tours to Switzerland, Italy and even Egypt through Thomas Cook and other firms.

Many Victorians, however, travelled for purposes other than leisure. Some emigrated to the colonies, particularly to Canada, Australia and New Zealand to start a new life. Thousands of Irish emigrants sailed to the United States after the potato famine of the 1840s, while others moved to England or Scotland. There was a constant flow of administrators, civil servants or missionaries going out to the expanding Empire, such as Maria Cust's husband in India. While some were leaving the British Isles, others were arriving, like the Jewish immigrants from Russia and Eastern Europe in the later Victorian period. Many Victorian travellers, whatever the reason for their journey, wrote about their experiences, often adding their own sketches of scenery and local characters as Andrew Donaldson did in Rome. Sketching, a common Victorian accomplishment, especially for young ladies, gave place to photography during the later part of the century. Photography began as an upper-class hobby requiring expensive equipment, considerable expertise and free time. By the 1840s, however, commercial studios were opening all over the country and before long many families could afford to have a group portrait taken. Many of our diarists mention going to the photographer's studio – the Pecks in Hertford, Maria Cust in London and the Donaldsons in Rome. As cameras became cheaper and simpler to use from the mid-1880s, people started to take their own 'snaps' on holiday and at family weddings and christenings. By the very end of the reign, Victorians might even have seen themselves on 'moving pictures', for the first public film shows were beginning in the late 1890s.

The importance of religion in the lives of our diarists may appear striking to the modern reader. For many, religious faith was a serious and important part of life, as it was for George Pegler, Arthur Peck, the Donaldsons and Amy Pearce. For others it may have been more of a formality; it is hard to tell. Science was a fascinating new world with great popular appeal, as George Pegler's diary shows. He and his friends enjoyed going to scientific lectures and demonstrations on up-to-the-minute subjects like electricity, and he was very interested in geological discoveries. His diary does not reveal his response to the publication of Darwin's *Origin of Species* in 1859, but the book shook the faith of many thinking Christians, at least for a while. Darwin's theory of evolution and new discoveries about geology showing that the earth was much older than the Bible stated, coupled with modern approaches to biblical scholarship, rocked the foundations of conventional belief. Church-going was the social convention – almost all the diaries mention it – but church attendance certainly declined from the 1870s.

Victorian Britain was, by and large, a law-abiding society, but the Victorian world was not immune to social misbehaviour. Pay levels were low, but alcohol was cheap, and drink led to criminal activity as well as widespread social deprivation. The setting up of the Metropolitan Police in 1829, soon followed by provincial city forces, resulted in country-wide coverage by the mid-1850s. The emphasis was on crime prevention. Police presence on the streets was quite effective in this, and popular with the middle classes. A reasonably efficient court system dealt with miscreants, who faced a harsh prison regime if convicted, and hanging for murder. Until 1852, depending on their offence, they might even be sentenced to transportation to Australia. Several of our diarists mention petty crime. Maria Cust catches local children stealing firewood, Joseph Hékékyan has his wallet stolen in Covent Garden, Arthur Peck sees an arsonist arrested, and Andrew Tait's teenage friends carry out some vandalism on the local sports field.

Throughout her reign, Queen Victoria served as a focus of national life. Before her the monarchy had been at a low ebb, for her uncles, George IV and William IV, had not been popular with the general public. Victoria's youth came as a novelty – as did the fact that she was a woman – and ensured much attention from the newspapers and magazines, which fuelled the considerable public interest in the royal family's activities. The queen's wedding, the birth of the children and their eventual marriages, the death of the Prince Consort Albert and Victoria's unpopularly lengthy mourning for him, her accession to Empress of India, the celebrations of her Golden and Diamond Jubilees and her death and funeral all provided chronological landmarks around which her subjects dated their own lives. Victorian diaries often mention some royal event and the public marking of it, like John Harley reading to his sister from the newspaper account of the Princess Royal's wedding in 1858, or Andrew Tait noting the future George V's wedding in 1893. And the queen herself was a great diarist, keeping a regular record from the age of 16 until her old age. The publication of a part of her diary, *Leaves from a Journal of Our Life in the Highlands* (1867), led to Disraeli's famous aside to her, one successful writer to another: 'We authors, Ma'am ...'

Diary-keeping was not, of course, a Victorian invention; it had been a popular pursuit since the 16th century. Some people kept a diary as an aid to their religious life, examining their conscience on a regular basis. This was particularly common among nonconformist and evangelical Christians, but not exclusive to them. Others kept careful memoranda of household or personal spending and began to add explanatory notes and other details of their daily activities to the same book. Still others began a narrative of their daily lives in mid-flow, though occasionally they recorded their reasons, such as needing a safety-valve for emotions best left unexpressed in public, with the chance to reflect on them later, in calmer mood.

None of the diarists in this book announces a special reason for starting a diary, though in some cases we can guess. Young Andrew Tait was about to move house, lose touch with his old friends and go to a new school. It seems likely that his diary served as a confidant through the transition. Maria Hobart was excited about her engagement and the preparations for her marriage to Robert Cust; she did not want to forget any of the enchanting details. Peter King was recording not only an unpleasant bout of hospital treatment, but his first meeting with his future wife. The other diarists probably wrote out of habit or (in the case of the curate and the nurses) because their work required them to. Whatever their reasons for writing, their personalities and views come through most clearly over one hundred years later. What strikes the modern reader forcefully is how little, in essence, life has changed. The diarists' concerns revolve around their own personal world, their families, friends, work and leisure. They do not, in the main, agonize over political events, moral dilemmas or the meaning of life. They are more concerned with a child's illness, finding a new house or problems at work. Births, marriages and deaths occur, we hear about domestic crises, schools and teaching, visits, shopping, Christmas, birthdays and – naturally – the weather.

Like us, the Victorians were a mixed bunch. Those who assume they were prudish may be surprised by Maria Cust's unwritten but clear anticipation of a happy physical relationship with her new husband, and by the fact that he attended the birth of their daughter. Not all Victorian fathers were chilly and distant tyrants. Leonard Wyon went shopping for baby clothes with his wife and often brought home little surprises for her and for the nursery. Andrew Donaldson was also a devoted family man. Arthur Peck rebelled briefly against his father's authority – he worked for him, as well as lived with him – but soon returned to the family hearth and seems to have stayed there for the rest of his life. Amy Pearce's father may have been sterner, but was no doubt provoked by his erring son whose debts he refused to pay. Possibly he sent Hugh away, but Amy's diary implies that the boy left home of his own accord. Family relationships were strong, and responsibilities keenly felt.

None of the diaries included here has been published before, with the exception of Peter King's, which was not widely circulated. This selection, the tip of a true iceberg of diary material available in record offices, libraries and museums here in Britain and abroad, gives a ripe flavour of life in the Victorian period and may help to rescue these Victorians at least from accusations of joyless repression and insular prejudice. Each diary is prefaced by a short biographical note about the writer and ends with details of his or her later life, if known. Many more diaries await discovery, with still more to tell us about the thoughts, concerns, feelings, relationships and day-to-day lives of ordinary men and women in a time of expanding horizons and rapid social change.

run while Aggie sat by me, then they returned for Lessons –
In the afternoon Aggie and I drove to St Stefano Rotondo. This is
one of the most interesting churches in Rome – Its circular form and
its colonnade of monolithic columns with larger ones in the centre are
its chief features – From thence we walked to the neighbouring church
of St Maria della Navicella, so called from the marble ship in the
piazza in front of it: This church has a remarkable mosaic in
the Apse containing a portrait of Pope Paschal 1st kneeling in front
of the Virgin – We walked through the Colliseum admiring
it's grand proportions seen so well in the glittering sun-light,
to the via Sistina where we visited Miss Pickering's Studio –
afterwards we called on Mrs Herriman – The children went to
the Villa Borghese and picked flowers

on the Pincio –

Sunday 6th Andrew & I went to the Early Communion at 8.31. Also
the children again to Church at 11 & Bessie went & I stayed with Dolly
& Baby. In the afternoon the little ones got out & we took the 3 Elder –
Jesuit to St Agostino where the 40 hours were being observed & then to
Vespers, sermon, (french) & Benediction at S. Luigi dei francesi –

A SKETCH OF THE VIEW FROM MONTE PINCIO IN ROME, FROM ANDREW DONALDSON'S DIARY

GEORGE PEGLER
Headmaster

George Pegler was a clever young man from the Stroud region of Gloucestershire. His family were shopkeepers, but he went into teaching, and by 25 (his age when the diary extract begins) he was Headmaster of the British School in Earith, Huntingdonshire. This, however, did not satisfy his ambition completely. He continued to study, later starting a new British School at Willingham, on the Cambridgeshire border, where he spent the rest of his teaching life. His busy social life revolved around the local Baptist chapels. In the school holidays he visited his brothers and sisters, who lived in London, and his relations in Gloucestershire. He was clearly an extremely earnest and conscientious man, suffering frequently from ailments which he sometimes attributed to overwork.

JANUARY 1 1850, TUESDAY ♦ Frosty. My sister came over from Colne today with Miss A. Stacey. They took tea and supper with me. I attended a lecture at the Institution Room on Electricity by Edw. Brown, but the machine did not work well from the dampness of the room.

JANUARY 2 ♦ My sister and Miss A. Stacey came over to see me again today. We went to the New Load Meeting to hear Mr E. Davis preach. He preached an excellent sermon, but it was read from a manuscript. Mr Smith supped with us this evening.

JANUARY 7, PLOUGH MONDAY ♦ I gave half holiday today and went with some of my boys skating on the fens and washes. My sister, Miss Walls, the two Miss Staceys and Miss Margarette and Eliza Tebutt came on the ice sliding. Miss Walls had a smart fall and hurt her face. They all came home to tea with the exception of Miss Eliza Tebutt. I went to the Missionary Prayer-meeting with some of the young ladies.

JANUARY 8 ♦ I went skating today for an hour. My sister called at my school-room today, in company with Miss Walls, Miss B. Stacey and Miss M.A. Tebutt. I met my Bible class this evening – but few attended.

GEORGE PEGLER, AGED ABOUT 75, WITH HIS WIFE MARIA

FIVE O'CLOCK TEA WAS POPULAR WITH MIDDLE-CLASS LADIES

JANUARY 13 ♦ This day I felt very unwell – did not go to Bluntisham before the evening.

JANUARY 14 ♦ I am much better in health, but I feel Spiritually unhealthy. May God in his mercy grant me his divine assistance. My School at this time is very trying, I have very many unruly boys come into my school now that they cannot do any thing out of doors. In the evening I went to a party at Mr Saunders at Bluntisham. Mr Simmons made himself very agreeable and was good company. Not being very well myself, and the weather was bitter cold, I accepted the kind offer of a bed at Miss Walls. I stayed at Wood End to breakfast. I have always found Miss Walls to be very kindhearted, and she possesses many of the finer feelings of our Nature. She has been very, very kind to my sister.

JANUARY 17 ♦ My sister and Miss Walls came to Earith this afternoon and took tea with me. I went to Bluntisham Meeting in the evening. I came home with Miss Jewson. Some ladies' minds are only pleased with light and trivial things, and like to read works of a like character in preference to works of stability, while I meet with a few others who go a step higher and like to talk about common place things, but not about any thing which requires penetration and continuous thought. This is to be lamented.

JANUARY 18 ♦ Today my Committee met to pass the year's accounts and consider a charge brought against me as the Master of the school, which was found to be groundless. Parents should be very careful how they spoke before their children, and if they wish them to improve in learning and moral feeling, inculcate obedience and respect for the Master.

JANUARY 21, MONDAY ♦ My school increasing. Mrs Gilleade came to the schoolroom this morning and humbly wished to have matters settled about her boys, which I think was done. In the evening I went to a party at Miss Simmons, Bluntisham. We were to be free from our accustomed frivolity at such parties, and to have singing &c instead of forfeits, but we did not refrain from our old games, and it gave umbrage to Miss Simmons, yet we closed the meeting by reading and prayer. I am fully convinced that there is too much lightness mixed up with those parties, it would be much better if there was more intelligence and refinedness of manner brought into these social meetings.

JANUARY 26–27, SUNDAY ♦ Very poorly. Mr Simmons preached a sermon this morning from these words "It is better to go to the house of mourning than to the house of feasting". He condemned our parties and what is called in them wit and 'cleverity'.

FEBRUARY 5 ♦ This morning my sister left for London after spending six weeks in Huntingdonshire. Miss Walls came with her horse and gig from Wood End by

¼ after 7 o'clock. We all breakfasted together and then went to meet the Train. I rode back with Miss Walls and B. Stacey.

FEBRUARY 11 ♦ This evening I gave a lecture on Gravity to our Intellectual Society.

FEBRUARY 25 ♦ I gave a lecture this evening on the Atmosphere to the members and friends of our Book Club and Mental Improvement Society. Two ladies present. They all appeared interested with what was advanced.

MARCH 15 ♦ I went to Bluntisham to hear Fisher the labourer give a lecture on total Abstinence, the School-room was full.

MARCH 24 ♦ I received a letter this morning with a watch guard enclosed in it, from a lady, intended as a birthday present. No name to the letter. I am very poorly today and have been for some days. At this time I feel very weak in Spiritual things, having but little peace of mind arising from a partial neglect of the Word of God and not being able to keep under my besetting sin, which is a cause of daily mourning and sorrow of heart. God help me.

MARCH 25 ♦ My birthday. I have now seen 25 summers. My years appear to pass quickly away. In the evening I met the members of our Book Club but little business was done.

George was less than satisfied with his lodgings, though he did not decide to move out until after Christmas.

APRIL 21, SUNDAY ♦ I am very unwell today. Have not been to Meeting today but stayed at home to nurse myself, having a very bad cold & cough arising from putting on damp linen. It was more the fault of my land-lady than myself. I shall be more careful in future about my linen. The weather is fine and seasonable – the gardens of plum-trees look remarkably well at this time. At this time Nature more especially shows forth her beauty and grandeur. Thoughts suggested by having my dinner ill-cooked and slovenly put on the table, plates &c barely clean: A pious, modest, virtuous, industrious and economic wife is a jewel, who will keep at home and attend to the concerns of the house, educate and train her offspring; teaching them lessons of piety, industry and modesty. Not indulging in bed until eight or nine o'clock in the morning and then get up to eat and drink, and after gourmandizing again retiring to bed for an hour after dinner – get up and prepare for tea – after which go to a neighbour's for a gossip and slander absent persons. I have seen this done while every thing is neglected at home, being left perhaps to an ill-trained daughter, who about half does what is intrusted to her.

BLUNTISHAM MEETING HOUSE – A NON-CONFORMIST CHAPEL WHERE GEORGE ATTENDED LECTURES

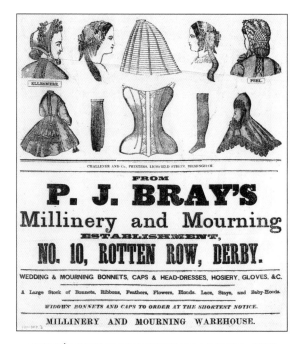

GEORGE'S SISTER WAS APPRENTICED TO LEARN MILLINERY

APRIL 23 ♦ This afternoon in consequence of a severe cold and cough caused first from putting on damp clothing, I clos'd my school and on the morrow I left Somersham for London. Miss Mary Sheebens accompanied me all the way. At Harlow I saw and spoke to Miss Ross, late School-Mistress of St Ives British School. While in London I visited the new House of Lords and attended at the House of Commons and heard debates from a little before five o'clock till nearly midnight. I was much interested.

MAY 29 ♦ Today I resolved to discontinue the use of the literal rod in my school. I shall dispense with corporal punishment in every form as soon as possible.

JUNE 6 ♦ The treat of the Bluntisham Sunday School. I went, but not to tea. We had a game at cricket for a time, but a heavy storm drove us from the field.

George's abolition of corporal punishment did not last long.

JUNE 10 ♦ Mr G. Mason gave a lecture in Bluntisham Meeting on Total Abstinence and Domestic Sanitary Reform. The lecture was very well attended, and gave general satisfaction. Some thought Mr Mason spoke too much in praise of himself. I now intend to enter upon the study of Latin steadily and if my health be spared I hope to succeed.

JUNE 14 ♦ For 15 days excepting Sundays I have put up my stick, hoping to do without corporal punishment in my school, but today I was obliged to bring it out again, but very reluctantly. I fear that I shall not be able entirely to dispense with the rod as long as the parents are so indifferent about good moral training at home. They furnish us with very unruly subjects.

JUNE 16 ♦ Mr Alport preached for Mr Simmons. He did not get on very well. He had closed his address by 20 minutes before 12 o'clock. Perhaps he will not be so forward to go into the pulpit again. Many persons very much dislike to see him there.

JULY 12 ♦ Young ladies are some trouble to me. I am much perplexed, but trust all will be for the Glory of God.

AUGUST 2 ♦ Three females were baptized by Mr Simmons at Bluntisham Meeting. This same evening a most awful accident occurred on the Colne Road when Mr John Butcher Senr. was killed and several others much injured. Mr Butcher was intoxicated.

AUGUST 9 ♦ This morning after putting things right in the school-room, we closed school at 3 o'clock and retired to Mr Brown's field and played a few games at cricket.

AUGUST 10 ♦ This morning I left Earith at ½ past 7 o'clock in Mr Brown's pony cart for the Somersham Station. Left at 8 o'clock for London, arrived in Town a little before two.

AUGUST 11 ♦ Today I visited the British Museum and confined myself to the inspection of Minerals. I saw Native Mercury in Quartz. Opalized wood from Van Dieman's Land interested me, and Bitumen in large lumps.

AUGUST 12 ♦ This day I went to the Polytechnic Institution and spent between 5 & 6 hours there. There were several objects which took my attention. The Electrical Eel was one.

The headquarters of the British and Foreign Schools Society was in Borough Road.

AUGUST 14 ♦ Rather cold and rainy. This day I went into the Boro' to purchase some books, but did not go into the Schools. Today the Queen prorogued the Parliament in person. I saw her carriage from the Strand. There was a great number of persons assembled to witness the procession, I saw a vast number of carriages.

AUGUST 22 ♦ This day was very fine and beautiful. I went to Gravesend today with my sister Dorcas, brother Alfred and cousin Rebecca. We went down by steam boats and returned by them. The day was delightful and the views from Windmill Hill were vivid and lovely. George and his brother travelled to Gloucestershire to see their family. He could not resist visiting the local equivalent of his own school.

SEPTEMBER 4 ♦ Paid Mr Webb a visit at his school and took tea with him. I questioned the boys on several subjects, they answered moderately, but the school was in first rate order, but not so high in knowledge as they were when I saw them a year ago. I met with a school Master at Mr Webb's with whom I was much pleased. We worked several problems in Algebra.

SEPTEMBER 14 ♦ Went to Stroud with my father in the afternoon, when we returned Father was very much disconcerted by hearing of an accident at the factory – he was not like himself for days – he allows little things to take so much effect on his mind. He did not go out to chapel on Sunday in consequence.

Back in Earith, George had a busy term.

DECEMBER 1 ♦ At this time I am much engaged to put my large school in order and to prepare it for Pupil Teachers. I am likewise hard at

Euclid and other studies in preparation for an examination for a Certificate of Merit.

DECEMBER 21 ♦ Today I went to London to see my brothers and sisters and to spend Christmas with them. I returned to Earith on the 28th and took up my abode at my new apartments – very comfortable. Mrs Horsford is very kind.

FEBRUARY 12 1851 ♦ Mrs Horsford married Mr John Wormsley. The wedding was kept at Mr E. Hodson's. Somewhere about 40 sat down to dinner and a greater number sat down to tea. I did not dine or tea with them being rather poorly, and had my school duties to attend to. Mr Smith came for me after tea and I spent the evening with them merrily. I did not like to hear song-singing. The Misses Harpers from Cambridge were very merry and cheerful. I enjoyed their society.

FEBRUARY 13 ♦ I was poorly after the feast. After all, all is vanity and vexation of spirit.

AUGUST 10 ♦ Visited London as is my custom, went to the Great Exhibition with my old friend Hapgood on Monday 12th and on Wednesday the 14th.

DECEMBER 16 ♦ Within the last two months I have been much put to. In the first place my bodily health and functions have been interrupted to some extent by the appearance of Boils. Again, my mind has been exercised in disappointment concerning school affairs. I have been reading with dilligence in preparation for an Examination for Certificates of Merit, but I have been foiled, my school being endowed to an extent as not to allow of my being examined at the "Annual General Examinations for Certificates". I am now in a strait betwixt two, whether to remain here or to leave this school and try for another. I have written to the Secretary of the British and Foreign School Society to know if I can obtain my Certificate from the Institution.

JANUARY 23 1852 ♦ I am sorry the Committee do not appear to be able to advance my salary, but they seem to be willing to do what they can for me. I now do not know what to do positively about these matters but trust to the Disposer of all events that all will be well. My school is full of boys, between 80 and 90 in daily attendance, 104 on the books – may feeble efforts be blessed to their eternal good.

FEBRUARY 26 ♦ Today M. Arnold Esq, HM Inspector of Schools visited my school for its annual examination. He arrived just before eleven o'clock, he should have been here at 10 o'clock. He took the Apprentice and Candidates into the Cloakroom and set them to work by themselves, while he heard the bottom drafts read and questioned them on what they had read and spelling. After they had read they were sent home for the day. He then examined the upper drafts in dictation on slates, then in reading, after that Arithmetic, not very well up in this branch – some of the elder boys were away. He then sent all home but those who learnt Grammar and Geography; he heard the two top drafts and the Pupil Teachers and Candidate. G. Gilleade took Geography and South Grammar, George was very slow and not very good, South was better in Grammar.

George went to Gloucestershire again during his summer holidays.

SEPTEMBER 9 ◆ Today in the afternoon I took my sister Eliza Pegler to Stroud to the Misses Bradford and Sage, Milliners and Dressmakers. We then and there came to an agreement that my Sister Eliza should serve them, the said Emma Bradford and Annie Sage, for the term of two years to learn the business of Millinery and Dressmaking as an Apprentice, for which I paid them the sum of four pounds sterling.

DECEMBER 23 ◆ From very close application to study I have been poorly for about two weeks. It is now near Christmas and I shall remain at Earith this Christmas, but have no thought of enjoyment in the sense of company or friends.

DECEMBER 25, CHRISTMAS DAY ◆ The dullest I ever saw. The day was very mild. I went into the Fens with Mr Edwards and his gun, but did not shoot much, as might be expected. I never had so bad a Christmas dinner in my life. The people of Earith do not think half so much of Christmas as they do of their Fair. Mr John Brown had his men wheat sowing on Christmas Day, others were at muck cart.

George renewed his acquaintance with the alluring Harper sisters, and soon became a friend of the family.

FEBRUARY 10, 1853 ◆ Today the Misses Harper and their eldest brother came to Earith to spend a few days with their aunt, Mrs Wormsley. We did not break up our party any evening until after midnight. Our games were very simple but most amusing, in truth they were so amusing that I shall not easily forget them, for they afforded much pleasure at the time, and they will be pleasantly remembered. My second impression of these young ladies is even better than the first. Their manners are easy and graceful; their behaviour bland and courteous to strangers, and to friends conciliatory, open and free, nothing constrained. They have a reverential regard for every thing sacred and divine, but nothing slavish about their religious concerns. They are excellent company.

MARCH 1 ♦ M. Arnold, HM Inspector of Schools, examined my school. He came by rail to Somersham and did not reach Earith until just 12 o'clock. I sent all the children home but the first two classes, those he examined in English History, Grammar, Geography and Arithmetic, and he said in my presence that he found my boys better acquainted with History and Geography than any schools he inspects.

MARCH 3 ♦ Today I took my Pupil Teachers to Cambridge to be examined in the British School-Room in Fitzroy St. I dined and tea-d at Mr Harper's in St Andrew's Street. I worked Mr Harper's Electrical Machine, we all had several shocks. My Friend Miss Harriette was from home with her mother on business.

MARCH 18 ♦ I read twice a week, to a few friends, Uncle Tom's Cabin.

MARCH 25, GOOD FRIDAY ♦ Today I am 28 years of age. Tomorrow I proceed to London to be ready for the Examination which will take place on Tuesday the 29th inst. I keep school today for the first time on Good Friday – only 26 boys present in the morning and 22 in the afternoon.

MARCH 26 ♦ On Tuesday evening I commenced my examination at the Boro' Road before Mr Morell. There was no difficulty in being admitted to the examination. The first paper was on Pedagogue, we commenced at 5 o'clock in the evening and left off at 8 o'clock. We finished our papers at 3 o'clock on Saturday afternoon April the 2nd. The papers on the elementary subjects were very difficult, such as Geography and History. The paper on Physical Science happened unfortunate for me for it had not a question on Pneumatics or Electricity. One or two on Magnetism, Galvanism and Optics. I was pleased with my Mathematical papers but had not time sufficient for either of them. I should like to have had more time for my Euclid paper. One question in Mechanics I might have done, but was tired. I am sorry I did not do it.

MAY 14, SATURDAY ♦ This morning I visited Ely with Mr Howard and ascended the tower of the cathedral and had a most magnificent view of the surrounding country, saw King's College chapel at Cambridge from that spot. We walked there and back; it was a beautiful day but I was very tired by the time I got home.

MAY 22 ♦ The Misses Harper, Mr P. Gray and Mr Oliver came over from Cambridge this morning and returned in the evening. In the afternoon we took a walk into the fields and in the evening performed an experiment making tables move round the room in the most remarkable manner by some unknown cause. I believe it to be by Electricity.

JULY 8 ♦ This morning about eight o'clock a terrible thunder-storm commenced and continued for about fifteen minutes. The rain came down in such torrents as to penetrate the best built houses; many persons were disturbed in their beds, for the water came down upon them profusely. The hail-stones were so large as to break the windows of some houses in Haddenham Fen. Mr R. Brown's crops in Haddenham Fen were very much damaged. The crops of others were also much injured.

JULY 12 ♦ I went to Houghton today and heard Mr Wittiker, Teatotaller from Scarborough, and Mr Jabez Inwards from Leighton Buzzard. The fireworks were good after the Meeting.

JULY 15 1854 ♦ Today, Saturday, my brother Henry and sister Maria came from London to Cambridge on their way to Earith. I went to Cambridge to meet them; we looked over Cambridge a little, walked through some of the College walks and came home in John Nail's market cart. They stayed with me a week. I believe they enjoyed themselves while here. They amused themselves with fishing several days; took some home to London with them.

AUGUST 12 ♦ Today I went to Cambridge to meet my sister Dorcas who was coming to see me for a few days; we walked about Cambridge a little while and then came to Earith with Mr Nail.

OCTOBER 12 ♦ My sister Dorcas was married today at Rodborough church (in Gloucestershire) to Mr John Beck of London.

George stayed at Earith until 1857, in spite of earlier temptations to move.

1857 ♦ Willingham, Cambs. I was backward and forward to Willingham for about three weeks before the School was opened for teaching. There was a public opening on the 13th November 1856 when more than 200 persons sat down to tea. After tea there was a public meeting at which Mr Charles Prentice Tebbut of Bluntisham spoke; in the course of his speech he was pleased to say that he "congratulated the Committee on obtaining the services of so excellent a Master" and if he, the Master, were not present he would say more of him, that is of course in his favour. This was very pleasing to me of course, coming from a gentleman who had known me for about ten years and from whom I had expected no such eulogy.

JUNE 7 1857 ♦ My school is going on very well, considering that I have been deprived of my expected Pupil Teachers. I have about 110 children in actual daily attendance. I devote but little of my time to study and reading at present. My amusement and recreation is chiefly at Quoits. The people whom I have at present associated with are what may be called with great propriety a good hearted people, they have been kind enough to invite me to many of their private family parties. I never feasted so much in my life in the time as I have since I have been at Willingham.

NOVEMBER 4 ♦ This evening I met as many of my elder pupils as felt disposed to come to the School-room to form an Elocution Class. 16 boys and 5 girls made their appearance and we had a number of recitations and it was altogether a very good beginning. We agreed to meet once a week.

George Pegler's troubles with unruly schoolboys whose parents were 'indifferent about good moral training at home' sound a familiar note to the modern reader. The Misses Harper, whom he found so charming, were nieces of his landlady and daughters of a Cambridge stay and corset maker. The 'M. Arnold' who came as School Inspector was the famous poet Matthew Arnold; George was, of course, especially proud of his satisfactory report on the British School in Earith. George taught at the British School at Willingham until his retirement in 1888. An ardent Unionist and staunch Liberal, he continued to live in the area until his death at the beginning of World War I.

LEONARD WYON
Chief engraver

Leonard Wyon was chief engraver at the Royal Mint, designing coins and medals as his father and uncles had done before him. He lived in St John's Wood, London, with his wife May and their baby daughter Edith. At the time the diary starts, August 1853, they had just returned from a lengthy seaside holiday. Wyon does write about his work, but mostly he concentrates on his home life, often mentioning his relations, including his brother Fred and sister Fan. May was prone to ill health, but Wyon seems to have been endlessly patient with her hysterical outbursts and was a devoted family man. The family was of German origin, and still had many contacts with Germany.

AUGUST 17 1853 ♦ Returned from Walton with May & Edith after a six weeks stay at the Sea Side, five of which were spent at Cromer. Framed some grand resolutions for which dear May laughs at me, and says I shall never carry them out – to write this diary is one, another is to be more methodical in business. We found our house and garden looking beautiful, May was in raptures. One or two letters, the only one of importance being from Sir J. Herschel asking my advice concerning the number of proof coins advisable to be struck.

AUGUST 18 ♦ Wrote a quantity of letters, unpacked medals and other things, then went to town. In the evening May & I had a walk and bought some things. Dear May has been very busy and as happy as a bird all day.

AUGUST 19 ♦ Commenced work today with really no great good will. Had a short walk with May before dinner. Fred who has just returned from his tour in Ireland, and Kullrich dined with us and spoke German all the evening. We all called on the Holts for a short time in the evening – they were very cold to us as we did not see their Baby before our summer's excursion, must make much of the little gentleman when we do see him. It appears from yesterday's Times that the Decimal Coinage has been finally agreed on, but the Public will probably be the losers by the exchange, especially in the smaller and consequently more important coins, such as the penny.

A PAGE FROM LEONARD'S DIARY

THE ROYAL MINT

This was one of many false starts before decimal coinage was finally introduced in 1971.

AUGUST 20 ♦ In the morning I worked for some time, and at 11 o'clock Kullrich commenced a model of me – at 3 o'clock May and I went to town to buy me a hat and other things, we walked home from the Pantheon. After dinner we had some music, Kullrich and May singing. I wish I could prevail on May to practise singing more. Read a very little of Esmond.

AUGUST 21, SUNDAY ♦ With May and Kullrich to Mr Fisk's church, but not, alas, to hear Mr Fisk who is away; instead a lisping curate and a feeble preacher who droned out a weak dilution of I John ch.2 v.1,2. In the afternoon we walked to Mr Webster's, who we were informed was away for a stay in the country for six weeks or so. Then to William Wratislaw's whose new house in Archer Terrace pleased us very much. In the evening we went again to church, after which May played Haydn & Handel.

AUGUST 22 ♦ A little walk with May; in the evening Fred came and we had plenty of music. May & I went out to look for a Laundress. Mrs Holt brought her little boy to see us, a fat boy.

AUGUST 24 ♦ Poor May has a very bad cold, she did not get up until 11. Kullrich and I went on with our models. At 3 we dined, and prevailed on Kullrich to stay another day, went for a walk with him in the evening. Fred came in the evening; he went to a theatre yesterday, scolded him for breaking his appointment with us.

AUGUST 25 ♦ May a little better. Modelled in the morning. Hurried Kullrich off in the afternoon for the Dover train, we are both very sorry he is gone.

AUGUST 28, SUNDAY ♦ May & I went to St John's church but we walked so fast that May was tired for the rest of the day. Heard Mr Dennis, the new Rector, preach a plain sermon.

AUGUST 30 ♦ May took Edith to Mrs Cooper's at Blackheath. I went to town: University College, Somerset House etc. Brought home a china candlestick & a melon for a surprize for dear May. Read to her in the evening, Moore's Fudges in England – good, but not nearly equal to the Fudges in Paris, also some of the Irish Melodies.

AUGUST 31 ♦ Mrs Brich & her son from Berlin called. She was an old friend of May's mother. Young Brich who I should think possesses no talent and certainly has no enthusiasm has just come to London from Berlin with the intention of setting up as a sculptor. They stayed an unconscionable time. When they were gone May and I walked through Regents Park to town, bought some Baby's frock-bodies and other things, walked home. Read Bleak House (part of the last number) to May.

SEPTEMBER 2 ♦ Another wet day. Poor dear May had hysterics, but I trust she is now quite well. Read the last of Bleak House to her in the evening.

SEPTEMBER 5 ♦ Nurse Mary went out for a holiday, so May had the management of Edith all to herself, in which she displayed great judgement. A little walk with May, read to her in the evening, the first act of Ben Jonson's Everyman in his Humour. Delighted with the nervous strength of the writing.

SEPTEMBER 6 ♦ Ormond Hill called this morning to ask me if I would draw a head of the Queen on a piece of steel for engraving for the new Receipt, declined it, not being in my way. He showed me what has been already done, which he says must be used at first till something good can be got to replace it. It is extremely bad, and I imagine will be much exclaimed against.

SEPTEMBER 7 ♦ At half past two May & I went to the Servants' Hall in Marlborough Street in search of a housemaid – saw several, but all to no purpose.

SEPTEMBER 8 ♦ May & I went to the Adelphi Theatre, saw To Parents and Guardians, a very good piece in which A. Wigan and Mrs Keeley played admirably; also Sardanapalus, a low burlesque which we were foolish for stopping to see, and The Camp at Chobham– very good, A. Wigan & Keeley being the principal performers. Surprized at the versatility of Wigan's talents which excel all other actors in this respect. Mrs Keeley's powers are incomparably superior to those of her husband, whose personal peculiarities (the lowest quality of an actor) are his principal attraction. Poor dear May was exceedingly drowsy during the last piece. I heartily wish we had left before it began, though it was a very good one.

SEPTEMBER 12 ♦ Mr Brown called at half past one, and ordered May some medicine which I sincerely trust may do her good. Afterwards we paid a second visit to Marlborough Street, and saw three wretched creatures as Housemaids. Next to the Lowther Arcade, Museum of Economic Geology.

SEPTEMBER 13 ♦ After lunch, May and I went to town for several matters. A servant called today from Marlborough Street with whose appearance we were very much pleased, so May will engage her (Caroline Burch).

SEPTEMBER 17 ♦ After dinner May & I went to Drury Lane Theatre to see Gustavus Brooke in Sir Giles Overreach – his acting of the last scene is fearfully real, an epileptic fit imitated with horrible minuteness. He is an actor of great powers, greater than those of any actor I have seen, but unfortunately a certain vulgarity will always prevent him from rising to perfection which – had he refinement of mind – he would certainly attain.

SEPTEMBER 18, SUNDAY ♦ In the morning May & I went to Lock Chapel, hoping to hear Mr Molyneux preach, but he being out of town his place was supplied by Mr Pattison, whose sermon impressed me more than any I have heard for a long time, notwithstanding that his style is always quaint and sometimes ludicrously so.

SEPTEMBER 19 ♦ Finished my drawing of May. It was a beautiful day, so after luncheon we called on Mrs F. Haggard and saw her Baby. It is now 2 months old but so small and withered that it appears to be at the point of death: it has a strange elfin likeness to Frederick Haggard.

SEPTEMBER 21 ♦ May took Edith and Mary to Fulham. Walked to Phillip's next door to the Pantheon to buy a Nursery lamp, some bottles etc. as a surprize for May when she came home. Walked home and arranged them in the bedroom. Read to May in the evening, the remainder of *Love's Cure*. Good, but not equal to any I have lately read. Some of the scenes sadly coarse, and I was at some trouble to make proper omissions.

Love's Cure *was by Beaumont and Fletcher, whose Jacobean frankness was too strong for Victorian tastes.*

SEPTEMBER 22 ♦ Dear little Edith was very unwell today. Wrote to defer our visit to Staines on account of Edith.

SEPTEMBER 23 ♦ Edith much better. May & I went to Phillip's to buy some things.

OCTOBER 21 ♦ Nothing occurred today except the visit of an old Captain Pope who called for subscriptions to the 'Distressed Needlewomen's Home'. He is a made up, longwinded old Captain.

Popular preachers drew crowds like modern pop stars. Day and Martin's was a brand of tea, with a well-known advertising slogan.

OCTOBER 23, SUNDAY ♦ To Christ Chapel in the morning, Mr Rich preached, afterwards we called on Uncle George. In the evening we went to Lock Chapel. As Mr Molyneux was to preach a great crowd was assembled at the doors more than half an hour before commencement of the service – some cracking nuts and jokes, and some squeezing. May heard a man close by us say to his friend (speaking of Mr Molyneux) "He's got a name, like Day & Martin, just the same". There was a great hustling and crushing when the doors were opened as at the pit of a theatre, and we had some difficulty in getting places.

Mr Molyneux preached an hour's sermon, and left no very favourable impression on us. His style is vigorous but without a particle of elegance, his utterance rapid to excess, which has probably contributed in no small degree to his fame for eloquence – and his action too great. On the whole he appeared to lack impressiveness, and we thought his powers were more those of an orator than a clergyman.

OCTOBER 25 ♦ May & Fan went to Shoreditch station to meet Fanny Atkinson. Poor dear May had a fit of hysterics – not so bad as usual, but her head was much worse afterwards.

OCTOBER 26 ♦ Dear May still far from well. May and I paid a visit to Mrs Hunt at the Governesses' Home, 66 Harley Street, to enquire if she knew any Family likely to suit Fan. She made an entry of it in her book & I have little doubt that she will assist us.

NOVEMBER 1 ♦ Mr Brown called today. He gave orders that May should not walk more than absolutely necessary and he changed her diet. Please God this may remove her hysterics.

NOVEMBER 3 ♦ Dear May had leeches on and remained in bed the greatest part of the day. She has been quiet and comparatively quite well. Her sofa arrived from Balls, with which she is much pleased.

NOVEMBER 5 ♦ A couple of riddles. What fur did Adam first wear? – Bare-skin. What kind of wind does a hungry sailor like best? A wind that blows foul (fowl) and then chops.

NOVEMBER 14 ♦ May still very unwell, perhaps worse, but Mr Brown gave her some medicine which did her a vast deal of good.

NOVEMBER 17 ♦ An event for May. Being a fine day I took her out in a Hansom Cab for a couple of miles on the Harrow Road. She had not left the house for a fortnight.

NOVEMBER 23 ♦ My Birthday, a grand day. When I woke dear May wished me many happy returns of the day in such a manner as would have been sufficient happiness in itself. There was a table at the bedside spread with presents: a purse from May, and Portemonnaie from Edith, a handsome prayer book from Fan and an inkstand from Fred. When I went into the Study I found that May had arranged my bench in the greatest order, and placed in the centre of it a vase full of flowers, on a very pretty mat a wreath of gold flowers on a green cloth ground – May's own invention. In my desk was a new book of blotting paper. After dinner we had dessert in the drawing room, and little Edith came down, dressed in her best and in full feather. Dessert was arranged in a most splendid manner, and all the Chintz had been taken off the chairs and sofa.

SIR JOSEPH PAXTON — DESIGNER OF THE CRYSTAL PALACE

WORKERS RESTORING MONUMENTS IN THE EGYPTIAN COURT OF THE CRYSTAL PALACE

DECEMBER 31 ♦ Mr Brown came – pronounced dear May much better. She has indeed been quite like her dear self yesterday, a happy omen I trust....

After its successful spell in Hyde Park housing the Great Exhibition, the Crystal Palace building was moved to Sydenham and reopened to the public. Its celebrated designer was Sir Joseph Paxton.

JANUARY 5 1854 ♦ To Sydenham by appointment to take Sir Joseph Paxton's portrait. In consequence of the heavy fall of snow the roads are in a horrible state. Omnibuses are very scarce and all drawn by 3 horses, & the charge is raised to 9d. Many cabs are drawn by 2 horses, enormous sums are paid. The papers say that there has not been such a winter for 17 years. I was fortunate in my drawing of Sir Joseph, with whom I was much pleased. He is a man evidently risen from the common class, but has thoroughly the look of a man born to do something and never to be curbed by difficulty. His manners are very agreeable & his face and head very fine, and particularly large.

JANUARY 12 ♦ Another sitting from Sir Joseph Paxton, this time for the model. Sir Joseph took me into the Crystal Palace, delighted with the Pompeian and Egyptian rooms which are nearly finished.

JANUARY 15, SUNDAY ♦ Dear May quite well! To Christ Church, heard a mad sermon from Mr Fisk.

JANUARY 19 ♦ Mr Brown called, and May being so well he 'dismissed himself'.

JANUARY 27 ♦ An excursion with May to West Drayton which we both enjoyed extremely: the object was to see if we liked the place sufficiently to look for lodgings there. It is a very rural place, which in fact is its chief charm, as it is not very practical for our purpose: we lunched at the inn close by the Railway & returned vastly pleased with our roaming in the country, which is such a change from our daily life.

MARCH 23 ♦ Dear little Edith's Birthday, she was in great force all day.

APRIL 15, EASTER SATURDAY ♦ At 2 o'clock we went to Mr Brown's. Started then in an omnibus which he had chartered, a party of 13, for Greenwich. Saw the Painted Hall & Chapel and also went into some of the Pensioners' wards. Afterwards visited the Kitchen and saw the tea brewing in coppers. A whitebait dinner at the Trafalgar and then home.

JULY 20 ♦ May was so annoyed by the unfeeling behaviour of our present nurse, Caroline, that she had hysterics – not a bad attack. I gave the nurse warning.

JULY 24 ♦ May had another fit of hysterics. A nurse called whom we shall most probably engage.

JULY 25 ♦ On arriving home we found several letters, one containing an unfavourable character of the aforementioned nurse.

JULY 29 ♦ A new nurse came this evening – Eliza Gardner. Caroline Bentley went previously.

Leonard and May set off for a summer holiday, leaving the baby with the new nurse.

AUGUST 4 ♦ May and I left home at 10 o'clock, but through a mistake in Bradshaw's Guide did not catch the train for Chepstow, we returned home and again started at 1 o'clock. Arrived at Chepstow at half past seven. Poor May is very tired, and to add to our misfortunes the principal hotel, the Beaufort Arms, had no bedroom for us, so we are obliged to sleep at a draper's over the way, a by no means satisfactory introduction to Chepstow. We had a walk in the evening.

AUGUST 5 ♦ We started this morning in a fly from Chepstow, having previously had a very nice walk in the grounds of Chepstow Castle, which are very beautiful. We arrived at Tintern Abbey at 12 o'clock, ordered dinner at a charming little rustic inn overgrown with roses and jasmine – again the Beaufort Arms – the name of most of the hotels hereabouts. We then entered the abbey ruins, and having formed magnificent ideas of them were rather disappointed, though its remains attest its former splendour: the place is kept exceedingly trim and neat, much to May's distaste, who approves of untidiness in ruins, but nowhere else. An excellent dinner at our model inn, and then on our road again to Monmouth. Our hotel is, of course, the Beaufort Arms.

AUGUST 6, SUNDAY ♦ Our Landlord told us that there are 2 churches in Monmouth: St Mary's, High church; St Thomas's, Low church. We went in the morning to the High church & were much disgusted with the entire performance. In the evening went to the low church with which we were much pleased.

AUGUST 8 ♦ We are now at the Angel Inn, Abergavenny. After tea, we walked out to see the town, a filthy place! I had no idea that England contained so foul a town. The inhabitants also seemed to partake of the degraded character of the place. We soon returned, heartily disgusted.

After a trip to Ireland, they returned to London and Edith ('quite well, but thinner'). Another baby was on the way.

SEPTEMBER 10, SUNDAY ♦ Dear May had felt unwell all day and at half past 8 was so ill that I sent for Dr Mackenzie and from thence to 38 Camden Street for Mrs Copland the nurse who was unfortunately out on an engagement. I then went for Martha, who sat up with dear May all night.

SEPTEMBER 11 ♦ This morning at half past 3 Baby was born, a little Boy – my dear Wife did not suffer so much as the last time. Dr Mackenzie recommended Mrs Acton of 4 Dudley Place as nurse; she came at half past 9. Emily, also the new Housemaid, came about the same time.

SEPTEMBER 30 ♦ Registered baby's birth.

OCTOBER 5 ♦ With May in a Cab to Hampstead. Passing through the Finchley Road we much admired the houses there & talked about looking for one there. To Uncle George's in the afternoon. He took me to a couple of houses in St John's Wood Park that I liked extremely. The rent of the house I liked so much is £130, and to be bought for £1800, Ground Rent £20.

OCTOBER 7 ♦ May & I went to see the house in St John's Wood Park. She was not so much struck by it as I was.

OCTOBER 12 ♦ At half past eleven o'clock went to the Rock Life Assurance Office, was examined medically by Dr Farre & met Uncle George there. Uncle George called in the evening & said that my proposal for Insurance at the Rock Office has been rejected, the reason assigned is that I am not sufficiently robust.

OCTOBER 16 ♦ Arthur was christened by the Revd. A. Taylor at Trinity Church.

OCTOBER 23 ♦ May had an explanation with the servants which ended with the dismissal of the nursemaid who had caused great disagreements among her fellow servants. My poor May was so much excited over it that after it was all finished she had a fit of hysterics which, however, were not bad and relieved her head.

OCTOBER 24 ♦ May very unwell in the morning. We called on Dr Mackenzie who we were gratified to learn did not apprehend that there was any real disease.

DECEMBER 18 ♦ Nomination day for the candidates for the Borough of Marylebone: I attended but not having taken my ticket with me as I ought to have done, was not admitted into the booth, and as it was a stormy day, raining occasionally, and the wind blew in violent gusts, I soon went away.

Elections were still very public affairs; the secret Ballot Act was not passed until 1872. Leonard had a vote, but of course May did not.

DECEMBER 19 ♦ Polling Day for the Marylebone election. Went to vote at Paddington Green, then I had a quiet morning's work and May read a good deal to me. After lunch we went out to see the state of the poll. Alas! Jacob Bell's numbers fell so far short of Lord Ebrington's that there was little hope: we walked to Grove Road Election Booth, and then May went home, and I to the central Booth at Park Crescent – there was a large mob there, cheering the supporters of Lord Ebrington and hooting those of Jacob Bell, and the Candidates themselves when they drove up a few minutes before 4 were received in like manner. I was extremely sorry for Mr Bell's failure.

DECEMBER 25, CHRISTMAS DAY ♦ Unfortunately the weather was worse than it has been for some time past, as it was hot and close besides continually raining. Dear May arranged a quantity of presents on the study table and all the servants after prayers went there, and Edith and Arthur were also brought. There were presents for everybody, not excepting Arthur, who received his with the greatest gravity.

AUGUST 13 1855 ♦ Last night we were kept awake the greatest part of the night by noises, which we imagined to proceed from next door, & therefore we sent a note in, in the morning, but the gentleman somewhat angrily replied that they were as much astonished at the noises as we were: doubtless they proceeded from the roof.

NOVEMBER 29 ♦ This morning we paid a second visit to a house in Hamilton Terrace, no 54, which we had seen when we first commenced our house-hunting, for on talking about it we came to the conclusion that it was more suited to us than any other we had seen. Our second visit gave us much pleasure, so I went to E. Burton to put the matter in hand, to send a surveyor, make the purchase etc.

FEBRUARY 10 1856 ♦ At half past 12 a girl was born, which proved to be so large a child that Dr Mackenzie weighed it on the meat scales, and found that it was as heavy as 9 ½ pounds. The size of the child caused dear May intense suffering which she bore heroically.

Great public celebrations were held at the end of the Crimean War. The Wyons decided to join in by decorating their new house.

MAY 29 ♦ Having heard that most people intended to illuminate their houses we bought half a dozen French lanterns which we fastened to the balconies on the first floor, but we found that illuminations in private houses, unless in the large thoroughfares and houses of people with note were the exception rather than the rule. At 8 o'clock May and I left home and endeavoured to get to Mr Fuller's in Piccadilly, but the crowd was so great, and the carriages so thickly packed in Oxford Street that we could not cross the road without going a good deal out of the way; we did this, therefore, and at last got safely to the other side, and then the way, when in Piccadilly, was comparatively easy: we went on to the roof and the fireworks almost immediately commenced, we were delighted with their magnificence, & saw not only those in the Green Park, to which we were close, but also Hyde Park, Primrose Hill & Victoria Park's. We supped at the Fullers & left at 12 o'clock, we returned up Park Lane. Baron Rothschild's illuminations (next to Apsley House) pleased us most, but we were struck with wonder at the sight of Lord Ward's: the outlines of the house and windows were all made out in gas besides other illuminations. The consumption of Gas was 2000 feet a minute.

AUGUST 17 ♦ Twice to Eaton Chapel: in the middle of it a man very near us had an epileptic fit and was carried out: it frightened dear May so much that she had the greatest difficulty in restraining hysterics.

JUNE 5 1857 ♦ This morning was rendered eventful by the birth of a son.

JULY 16 ♦ Eliza took the baby to Dr Mackenzie, and alarmed us a good deal with his report of his precarious condition.

JULY 17 ♦ Our charwoman went early this morning for a person to act as wetnurse for the child, but as no good arrangement could be made with her we went to the Lying In Hospital and procured a wet nurse there.

As his family increased, Leonard's diary entries grew shorter, relating mostly to work.

MAY 23 1864 ♦ I had a sitting from the Prince of Wales. The Princess came into the room & I had some talk with her. She is remarkably thin & her features, in a quiescent state have not much beauty, but when they are lit up by a smile her face becomes lovely. She seemed very gentle, timid and sweet – less royal than any great person I have seen.

Leonard, May and his family lived on in the same house in St John's Wood until he died. He engraved dies for the British military and naval medals issued between 1851 and 1891, as well as the medal issued to commemorate the Princess Royal's wedding in 1858. The medal for the 1887 Queen's Jubilee, which he engraved to someone else's design, was criticized when it appeared, and his dismay is said to have hastened his death in 1891.

MARIA CUST
Mother

Maria Hobart was 18 when she met her future husband, Robert Cust, and 23 when they married in 1856. Robert was a barrister and home on extended leave from the Indian Civil Service. Both came from well-connected clergymen's families and had aristocratic relations. It is clear from Maria's diary that both families were delighted with the engagement, which was regarded as entirely suitable. Maria lived in great comfort at 61 Eaton Square with her widowed mother and her sisters Louise and Sophie. Her two brothers, Bob and Bertie, visited frequently. Bertie was about to go into the Army. The family also had a country house at Langdown, near Southampton. The diary begins with Maria's engagement and wedding plans.

MARCH 1 1856 ♦ Walked with Aunt Mary Jane to look at apartments. Lunched with Aunt Edmund & afterwards went to see Mrs Pepys. My dearest Robert came to see me. He proposed the fixing of our Wedding day to Mamma, & asked her to tell him about her Lawyer &c. We talk of the 10th of May but things may occur to alter it, but that will probably be the day, & I look forward to it with the greatest happiness when I shall be united to the one whom I love best upon earth. (God grant it may not be too well!) My dearest, dearest Robert!! (10 weeks)

MARCH 3 ♦ A long happy chat with my dearest Robert.

MARCH 6 ♦ Uncle John came in to luncheon & also Aunt Mary, with whom and Aunt Edmund I went out driving. Dined at Miss Cust's (30 Hill Street) to meet Regd. and Ly Elizabeth & my dear Robert. I expected to have been very Shy, but the kindness of my future Aunts caused me to pass a very pleasant evening.

MARCH 8 ♦ Walked alone in the morning and with Sophie in the afternoon but we were picked up by Aunt MJ & Mamma & had a stuffy drive in a Clarence. Aunt Mary Jane gave me a gold brooch to match the earrings she had so kindly given me on the 29th February – one week gone! Nine still remain. Mamma wrote to request the Bishop of Worcester to perform the Marriage Ceremony on the 10th of May.

MARIA CUST'S DIARY

A NEW BABY WAS CARED FOR BY A NURSE IN WELL-TO-DO FAMILIES

MARCH 9, SUNDAY ♦ Went twice to St Michael's church. Mamma went in the afternoon & my dear Robert joined us there. He came home with us, and we had an hour "tête a tête". The Bishop of Worcester consents to unite us on the 10th of May.

MARCH 10 ♦ Received a letter from Uncle John enclosing a cheque for £50 to be expended in a Veil &c, such a kind present!

MARCH 11 ♦ Drove with Mamma in the morning. We chose the Brussels lace Veil and flounces given me by Uncle John and Aunt MJ. Dearest Robert came to see me in the afternoon.

MARCH 12 ♦ Mamma gave me a Spanish mantilla & flounces, & we paid for the White Lace.

MARCH 20, MAUNDY THURSDAY ♦ We all went to St Michael's church. On our return found the person whose advertisement we had answered waiting to be seen. Sarah Barnham, of Acton, Middlesex, a travelling Lady's Maid. (Memo. to see her again). My dearest Robert in London for the morning & came to see me. He & I, with Bob and Sophie, went to look at lodgings & saw Nos 4 & 2 Wilton Street, each 3 guineas per week and also 35 Chapel Street – 6 guineas per week with "Buttons" included, these last were spacious apartments.

MARCH 23, EASTER SUNDAY ♦ Bertie came home to breakfast. We all went to St Peter's church & (with the exception of Sophie) all received the Holy Sacrament, probably for the last time all together, as Whit Sunday (7 weeks hence) will find me, I trust, the wife of my dearest Robert! The Bishop has offered to find out whether we can or cannot be married at St Peter's church.

MARCH 27 ♦ My dearest Robert came up from Windsor for the day & came to see me in the afternoon. We all four went with him "lodging hunting" saw several in Half Moon Street, especially liked one kept by the servant of the late Lord Raglan, a German by name Roth, with a French wife, No. 40.

MARCH 28 ♦ Five hours of a Clarence with Mamma, got through 12 visits besides 2 others to get the character of Sarah Barnham.

MARCH 29 ♦ Engaged S. Barnham to come to me on April 30th as my maid.

APRIL 5 ♦ This day 5 years ago commenced my acquaintance with my dearest Robert.

APRIL 18 ♦ At ½ past 10 am Bertie and I set off to walk to Duke Street to call for dear R. We then took a cab to Hungerford Market. Got on board the 'Bride' 2d steamer to Paul's Wharf where we took the 'Daylight' to London Bridge. Went down by the 12 o'clock train to Woolwich, walked from the Station & arrived at the Pagets at ¼ before one o'clock. Immediately after luncheon Georgy, Leo, Harold & Claude set off with our trio to the Arsenal, where we saw the Russian trophies & then went thro' all the workshops, ending with the Lancaster Shell factory; being too late for the train, we determined to return by water & went off in a little boat to catch the steamer, which we just managed to do – the height from the boat to the steamer was such that I know not how I should ever have got on board had not Robert lifted me up in his arms. We had a charming voyage to Hungerford pier, where after a good deal of indecision we determined to wait for the boat to Pimlico pier, from whence we walked home where we arrived at 7.20. Robert stayed to dine with us, impromptu.

APRIL 22 ♦ Sophie confirmed with many others by the Bishop of Oxford, who gave a most impressive charge. Bertie received a letter from Genl Lewis to tell him that he must pass another examination in Mathematics before he receives his commission.

APRIL 26 ♦ Robert came & took me to see Mrs Harry Cust, met Lord Kilmorey there, the second time of my seeing him. Was introduced to Mrs Cuthbert in her bedroom, her baby being only 14 days old.

APRIL 28 ♦ Robert came later than he promised being very unwell, but we went to look at lodgings in Lr Belgrave St & Wilton Place. The anniversary of my first seeing dear Robert on his return from India last year.

APRIL 30 ♦ My new maid Sarah Barnham came £16 per annum wages, £5 per annum washing.

MAY 1, ASCENSION DAY ♦ Went to St Peter's church and received the Holy Sacrament with Mamma, Louise & Sophie for the first time. Dear Robert came after luncheon and brought me an Indian shawl, a present to him for his wife from Mr Seton Karr. Robert's old nanny from childhood days, still with the Cust family, was included in the wedding celebrations.

MAY 2 ♦ Went to 4 Chapel Street to ask the old nurse, Mrs Partridge, to come to our wedding.

MAY 5 ♦ Went to Mr Lintott dentist and had one tooth stopped.

MAY 8 ♦ The tenth anniversary of my dear Father's death. Attired myself in my "robe de mariage" for Robert's edification.

MAY 9 ♦ Robert came for me and took me out walking, or rather in a cab, to Abud jeweller in Conduit St and then to Hill, Regent St where we met Bob, assisted Robert to choose a scarf and he then gave me over to Bob's care & we returned home to luncheon. Went with Mamma & Louise in the carriage to choose a travelling box &c. At 5pm Robert came, then Harry and Reginald Cust, Henry Pepys and Mr Steward, the lawyer, for the signing of our marriage settlements.

The sun shone brightly as we signed our names, the first time it had done so in the course of the day. I was dead tired & could hardly hold up my head all the evening.

The wedding day arrived at last, and after the ceremony the honeymoon couple travelled to Robert's father's country estate at Cockayne Hatley in Bedfordshire.

MAY 10 ♦ Awoke at six o'clock, feeling almost ill with nervousness and fatigue. Breakfasted all together at 8 o'clock, & at ten commenced my toilette. At ½ past eleven o'clock left 61 Eaton Square with my dear Mother. On our arrival at St Peter's church we had some difficulty in being allowed to enter by the Vestry door. Sir G. Tyler & Uncle Edmund came out to meet us and in the vestry we found Mr Fuller & my eight bridesmaids, viz Louise & Sophie, Eleanor & Georgy Cust, Charlotte & Jane Astell, Harriet Gosling and Louisa Cameron. We immediately proceeded into the church where all were assembled and before the clock had struck 12 I was united in the bonds of Matrimony to my long loved Robert. After registering our names we returned to Eaton Square in Miss Cust's carriage. The party quickly assembled and after some little delay we went up to Breakfast in the drawing rooms. The rooms were crowded & everything went off as well as possible. The Bishop proposed our healths, to which Robert responded. There was tremendous cheering after each speech. I remained in the room till all was over & then went to change my dress. Left Eaton Square with my dear Husband in Miss Cust's carriage and went to Hill St to see Mr Cust and the Misses Cust, stayed till four o'clock when upon partaking of coffee we started for King's Cross where we found the maid and luggage. 5 o'clock train to Sandy, carriage and post horses to Cockayne Hatley which we reached at 7 o'clock & found the bells ringing & the school children cheering. We walked out to speak to them and dined at ¼ before 8 o'clock. A very very happy day & bright throughout. May God grant that it may be but the beginning of many happy years to us both and may He assist me to fulfil those vows of duty and obedience to my husband which I this day made.

MAY 11, SUNDAY ♦ Attended the morning service at Hatley church with my dear Husband. Walked into the village to see some of the poor people. After tea Robert read the Evening Service to me.

MAY 13 ♦ Drove to Potton and Gamlingay. Walked down to the village to see the Fair, which consisted of one gingerbread stall only. Robert invested 6d for the benefit of the children who came flocking in, almost as soon as he appeared near the Stall.

MAY 22 ♦ The Feast to the parish. Saw 14 puddings boiling in the copper in the Brewhouse! The party sat down to dinner in the coach house, 63 in number, at 4 tables: the good cheer consisted of two rounds of beef, 25 lbs each, two legs of pork, 17lbs each, and a leg of mutton, vegetables, pudding and ale. We saw the whole party set to work, we then left them for about ½ an hour and then returned for the toasts. R made a charming speech in returning thanks for our healths. After the dinner was over some of the people began to dance notwithstanding the wet state of the grass, and the boys were set to climb a soapy pole for a leg of mutton which proved quite unsuccessful, they then dived for oranges and apples & immediately after buried their faces in flour to pick up a bullet. After which jumping in sacks was the order of the day, concluding with tossing in a blanket. Everybody was highly amused & regretted that Mr Cust "had no more sons to marry". All the fun was arranged by Rt himself.

MAY 27 ♦ Left Hatley and ended our happy honeymoon, much to our regret.

Maria and Robert were in Hyde Park to see the celebrations marking the end of the Crimean War at exactly the same time that Leonard and May Wyon were watching from Piccadilly, as Leonard notes on page 32.

MAY 29 ♦ Rt and I went up to London. Walked from Paddington to Eaton Sqre where he left me till 7 p.m. when he came to fetch me to see the fireworks in Hyde Park, of which we had a capital view from a stand for which he paid 1/6d apiece.

JUNE 4 ♦ This day was the anniversary of the mutual recognition of attraction between my dear Rt & myself.

JUNE 13 ♦ Went to the Lyceum Theatre to see Madame Ristori act 'Maria Stuarda' in the piece of that name. She is a wonderful tragic actress but I hardly like her so well as Mlle. Rachel.

JUNE 26 ♦ Bertie came to luncheon & to go with us to the Crystal Palace Flower Show. Dined there, and came home to tea. Went to Aunt Edmund's Ball!

After a Continental tour, the newlyweds settled down to married life in Windsor and London, but 1857 was to prove a difficult year.

JANUARY 1 1857, THURSDAY ♦ Another year opens upon me, but in a different aspect from the last, then all was uncertainty, now my fondest hopes & wishes

THE GREAT EASTERN STEAM SHIP

AFTER BEING SEIZED BY MUTINEERS ON MAY 11, DELHI WAS RECAPTURED BY THE BRITISH

are realized, and I find myself the happy wife of one of the best of men & fondest and most devoted of husbands – God grant this happiness may long continue.

FEBRUARY 20 ♦ At Reading we had to wait 2 hours. Walked about the town for the first hour, during the second we were both weighed. Robert, 14 st. 5 lb., I, 8st. 4 lb.

MARCH 2 ♦ Walked all the morning. Had my hair cut. Hired a piano forte & commenced subscription to Music Library for 3 months.

MARCH 14 ♦ Mr & Mrs Brandreth having got an order to see the Electric Telegraph at Lothbury, called for us to go with them. It was a very curious and interesting sight. The Inland clerks are almost all young women. After this we went to the Bank of England, Royal Exchange, Lincoln's Inn Hall & Library, & Covent Garden Market.

MARCH 16 ♦ Passed the morning in the British Museum, my first visit. Went in the evening to the Princesses Theatre to see Richard 2nd which is splendidly got up, but being the second piece it lasts so late that we could not stay. I was unlucky enough to be so faint as to have to retire into fresh air and in so doing lost one of my Florentine bracelets.

Maria was now suffering some symptoms of early pregnancy.

MARCH 25 ♦ Riding put a stop to, much to my regret, but I suppose it is all for the best.

APRIL 2 ♦ My photograph taken by Claudet.

Antoine Claudet was a 'daguerrotype artist' at 107 Regent Street.
The horrifying details of the Indian Mutiny shocked everyone, especially those with Indian connections, like the Custs and the Hobarts.

MAY 27 ♦ The telegraph brought the sad news of the Mutiny in India and the capture of Delhi. Robert much distressed.

MAY 29 ♦ The Indian mail came in with full details of the Mutiny. Robert was absent all day at Haileybury College for the half-yearly examinations and in the evening he was at the Law Amendment. He came back with very bad news, as he heard that all Military officers on furlough had been ordered out and probably all Civilians would be ordered out also in consequence of the confusion in India. This made us both very unhappy.

JULY 1 ♦ We knew that the question of sending out the Civilians would be decided today and we were in great suspense: great was the relief brought by a letter that the decision was suspended untill the arrival of the next Mail.

JULY 6 ♦ By steamer to Blackwall: a heavy shower caught us at London Bridge: went over the Surrey and Windsor Castle in the East India Docks, in which Capt. and Mrs Brown and the Brothers Hobart and their wives are to start for Calcutta and Bombay. The latter ship is very comfortable. We then went on board the Agamemnon, a first rate man of war, in the hold of which the cable of the new Atlantic telegraph is being coiled: this is a wonderful sight, the rope is paid in from the shore and coiled round a bulkhead. We had also seen the Great Eastern Steam Ship on our road down, but did not go on board. Dined on whitebait and a bottle of champagne at Greenwich: this was my first experience of this kind of thing.

JULY 15 ♦ Bertie is first for service. Robert is very anxious about his own fate, the details of the Indian news are dreadful.

JULY 16 ♦ The post came early and brought Robert news that the Directors had abandoned the idea of sending out the Civilians, this was good news for us.

Maria and Robert spent an unsettling autumn wondering if and when Robert would be sent to India, and awaiting the birth of their first child.

OCTOBER 17, 7.45 A.M. ♦ Symptoms showed themselves which prevented my going down to breakfast. Dr Bullar was sent for & ordered me to bed there to remain tho' not feeling at all ill. Mamma slept in my room.

OCTOBER 18, SUNDAY. 8.30 A.M. ♦ A slight pain caused a note by fly to be dispatched post haste to Dr Bullar. The pains increased in frequency and severity. Dr B arrived at 11.40 & at 12.20 our little one was brought into the world & cried out loud. There being no nurse, Horton and Ann (housemaid) had to wash & dress the infant, who was pronounced to be a fine child, but sometime afterwards was considered very small indeed. She was born with dark hair & beautiful nails on her hands and feet. Dear Rt was allowed by Dr B to be of the greatest comfort to me in supporting me during the last pains. I was ordered to be kept very quiet but nevertheless saw my sisters in the evening. The baby was brought to me several times in the day and night but not allowed to remain. At the time of the birth there were present Dr B, Robert, Mamma, Horton and Caroline.

OCTOBER 19 ♦ The nurse arrived at 8 a.m. & was horrified to find the baby had had no food. Dr B came in the middle of the day, all well. Mr Gray came to name the baby – Albinia Lucy, after her two dead Aunts.

OCTOBER 21 ♦ Dr B not so well satisfied from the sudden flow of milk which made me very uncomfortable. The nurse put on oil silk.

OCTOBER 26 ♦ Baby growing, but very very small. All going on well. Pheasant and hot sherry and water. 9th day.

NOVEMBER 3 ♦ At 8.45 the baby was suddenly seized with rattling in her throat, having been taken from her cot apparently well. Mamma was called & she was to all appearance almost suffocated. Mrs Crowder loosened her clothes and rubbed her chest and back while Caroline held the candle close to her eyes which made her cry and sneeze, which relieved her. Mamma rubbed tallow on her forehead and after ¼ of an hour she was brought to me, terribly altered in countenance but a moderate meal brought her more to herself, and she had no other attack. The cause was supposed to be that after sucking, 2 hours before, she had been sick, & thrown up the milk into her head, & on awakening all the passages for breath were closed.

NOVEMBER 17 ♦ Mrs Crowder, monthly nurse, left us.

Robert learned that he would, after all, have to return to India and his administrative duties with the East India Company, and the pleasure of the new baby was mixed with anxiety as he prepared to leave.

NOVEMBER 30 ♦ Robert took his baggage over to Southampton to be shipped to Calcutta. This does indeed look like going!

DECEMBER 5 ♦ Thoroughly uncomfortable & nervous. Albinia Lucy was received into the Church by Mr Canning at St George's Chapel & duly registered. There was a christening breakfast and a large cake with a candle on the top!

DECEMBER 6 ♦ Received the Holy Sacrament with my dear Husband for the last time before his departure for India. God grant we may again kneel together at His altar!

DECEMBER 10 ♦ Baby weighed in her night clothes after deducting their weight she was found to be 7lb 6oz.

DECEMBER 20, SUNDAY ♦ The last day together. Both of us sadly out of spirits and I so nervous I could not sit through the dinner tho' I came in again for the dessert & touched glasses with dear Rt. He finally arranged all papers to be left with me, gave me his watch & paper of wishes to be executed. He gave me a bracelet of his hair as a Xmas gift & also the second cameo brooch as a wedding day present for the next 10th May.

DECEMBER 21 ♦ A sad sad day for us both. We got up at 7 a.m., said our prayers together for the last time for many long months. Rt had his breakfast & then took leave of the baby. We both wept bitterly especially dearest Rt when the moment of parting came – at 8 o'clock. Bob drove him off in the pony carriage. I rushed to the back stairs window and saw him wave his handkerchief as long as he was in sight, & then went sadly back to bed.

DECEMBER 22 ♦ A heart-broken letter from dear Rt written from Dover just before embarking. Wrote to him again at Trieste.

DECEMBER 25, CHRISTMAS DAY ♦ The church ringers came at 8 o'clock, a vile performance owing to the clerk's detestable vanity.

1858 was a depressing year for Maria as she waited for letters from Robert and hoped that she would soon be able to join him.

JANUARY 5 1858 ♦ Dr Bullar came to vaccinate the baby. She cried a great deal and her arm, which was punctured in three places, bled a good deal, but she went to sleep afterwards.

JANUARY 12 ♦ Woke with a cold and sore throat. Dr Bullar came to the baby & pronounced her to have taken the infection most vigorously. He ordered mustard and linseed poultices to my throat, gargle of tepid water & to stay at home.

JANUARY 13 ♦ Poor Baby's arm in a highly inflamed state from the shoulder to the point of the elbow, & so painful she could not bear it to be touched. Tepid water bandages however were of great use as well as sponging.

JANUARY 14 ♦ Baby's arm better though still much inflamed and heated. Waller tried to give her some Magnesia but she would not keep it down.

JANUARY 20 ♦ Walked out twice. S & I caught 4 children breaking & carrying off wood. We got their names & captured the faggot with their ropes.

JANUARY 21 ♦ Police Constable Jones says S or I must appear for the prosecution if anything is to be done to the children we caught yesterday & as we can't do that, it must be let alone.

MARCH 1 ♦ At last got a letter from my dearest husband dated from Madras Jany 24th.

MARCH 15 ♦ Watched all the morning for the annular Eclipse of the sun about which so much fuss has been made & missed it at last being only aware of it about 1 o'clock, a few moments after which it cleared into a bright afternoon.

JUNE 5 ♦ Dear Rt's first letter from Lahore arrived, no. XXIV, announcing his arrival & full of plans for our coming out to him. God grant our wishes may be fulfilled & we may be together by Xmas at last!

By September, Maria was making travel arrangements and staying near Dover.

SEPTEMBER 5 ♦ Alba crawled across the room for the first time. Took A out in the perambulator while Waller was at church – she would pull off her hat perpetually to the great amusement of everyone on the Parade.

SEPTEMBER 7 ♦ Rode up to Beachy Head & got a capital gallop on the Downs.

SEPTEMBER 9 ♦ Rode up to Beachy Head in the morning had a horse sixteen hands high but so small a saddle I could get no seat in it, fortunately the lady who rode with me did not wish to go fast.

SEPTEMBER 18 ♦ Went to the P & O office, & over the Ripon, not at all satisfied with the cabin allotted to me.

OCTOBER 4 ♦ Bob escorted me to London by early train, found Aunt MJ awaiting me at the Grosvenor Hotel. Went to the P & O office in Leadenhall Street about my cabin, &c &c.

OCTOBER 8 ♦ My new nurse Holding came.

OCTOBER 18 ♦ Our darling Alba's 1st birthday. We weighed her & measured her, weight 19 lb, height 2'3" and a ½.

OCTOBER 25 ♦ Left Langdown by 10 o'clock train for Southampton. Went on board the Ripon at 1 o'clock & got my cabin the Admiralty Agents arranged. Took leave of all my dear relations ... not least my kind brother in law, Harry Cust, who has been a true brother to me. At 2 pm we steamed out of dock waving our handkerchiefs eventually even Alba trying to do the same.

Maria sailed off to India, where she settled in Lahore with her beloved Robert. She died in 1864, to Robert's obvious distress, who read through her diaries and added his own sad comments here and there. Where she mentions having her photograph taken by Claudet, the Regent Street photographer, he adds 'a daguerrotype in a small case which I have always by me'. When she notes that she must stop riding because of her pregnancy he explains 'My dear wife consulted Dr Locock who ordered it'. With her diaries is a sketch plan of their house in Lahore, on which he has marked a bedroom, 'In this room my sweet wife died'. Robert married twice more, and lived on until 1909. His own diaries are in the British Library (Add. Ms. 45,400), and in them we meet Albinia Lucy again, sturdily outperforming her timid brother at riding school. She must have taken after her mother, who loved to ride.

JOHN PRITT HARLEY
Actor

John Pritt Harley was a well-known comic actor, famous above all for his Shakespearean roles, although he also had great success as Bob Acres in Sheridan's The Rivals. *A tall, very thin man, he was jokingly known as 'Fat Jack'. Perhaps he had always kept diaries, but this is the only one known to have survived. When he wrote it – in 1858 at the age of 70 – he was in regular employment at the Princess's Theatre, Oxford Street, where the manager was Charles Kean, and received the considerable salary of £10 a week. In his neat, precise writing he recorded a great deal of information, every day, in a small space: household expenses, rehearsals and performances, daytime activities, and especially his meals, in which he was clearly very interested indeed. He lived at 14 Upper Gower Street with his sister Betsy, cook Anne and housemaid Sarah. He gave Betsy £4 a week for the housekeeping. Harley liked the fine things in life, often noting the source of gourmet food or the maker of his new clothes.*

JANUARY 1 1858, NEW YEAR'S DAY ♦ I gave my Dear Sister Betsy a new Pocket Book. Lots of luck and God bless us both, and all we love, and all who love us, and God bless and prosper all our arrangements through the coming year. Arose half past eight. Breakfast half past nine. Theatre at 12 no rehearsal for me. Note from Mr Groom, Garrick Club at two, met E. Cooke, J.C. Deane, Brasseur, Sir C. Ibbetson. Home quarter to three. Dinner at four, mutton chops, potato, pheasant, boiled plum pudding, biscuit, cheese, ale, brandy, port and sherry, tea at seven to theatre at nine & back, read Spectator to Betsy, supped at eleven, cold pheasant, biscuits, cheese etc, cake, brandy and water. Read Tatler to Betsy, bed quarter before one.

JANUARY 2, SATURDAY ♦ Arose at half past eight, breakfast half past nine, theatre at one met Ellen in Box Office, home at two, Garrick Club at three, met J.P. Cooke, Copeland, Buckstone, C. Reade etc. Dinner at five, roast mutton,

JOHN PRITT HARLEY, AS TONY LUMPKIN, ONE OF HIS FAMOUS ROLES

PLAYBILL FROM THE PRINCESS'S THEATRE, WHERE HARLEY PERFORMED

OXFORD STREET, SHOWING THE PRINCESS'S THEATRE

potato, biscuit, cheese, ale, port and sherry. Tea half past six, in buss at seven to Haymarket Theatre, saw Speed the Plough and pantomime Sleeping Beauty, met Howe and son in Dress Boxes, home in Buss at twelve, supped cold mutton, biscuit, cheese, ale, gin and water, bed half past one. Paid Anne the cook a quarter's wages, due Jany 3 £3.00.

JANUARY 3 ♦ Arose at half past eight, breakfast quarter before ten. Did not attend Divine Service. Read and wrote lessons at home, Garrick Club at three, met J.P. Cooke, Shirley Brooks and Leigh Murray, home at half past four. Mrs Armstrong and Mary called. Dinner half past five, boiled mutton, potato, roasted hare, biscuit, cheese, ale port and sherry. Tea half past seven, walked at half past nine twice to Gt Russell Street, Bedford Square, home half past ten, read Spectator to Betsy, supped at eleven. Cold mutton, biscuit, cheese, gin and water. Bed at one. Mademoiselle Rachel died near Cannes aged 37.

JANUARY 4 ♦ Arose half past eight, breakfast half past nine. Went to Regent Street & saw John Savory and his son Charles. Then in buss to Southwark Street, saw Mat and her mother and J.C. Harding. Rehearsal at two, home to dinner at four. Roast beef, potato, biscuit, cheese, ale, port and sherry. Tea at seven. Left letter of excuse and card at J. Cooke's on having to decline dining with him tomorrow. Theatre at eight, saw Ellen on stage. Home at ten, supped at eleven, cold roast beef, biscuit, cheese, ale, gin and water. Read Spectator to Betsy. Bed at one. C. Kean ill, unable to act Hamlet.

JANUARY 5 ♦ Two ton coal today. Arose at half past eight, breakfast half past nine, rehearsal at twelve, home half past three. Dinner at four, roast mutton, potato, biscuit, cheese, greens, ale, port and sherry. Tea at six, theatre half past six. Met Ellen in Green Room, acted in one piece, home half past ten. Supped at eleven, cold roast beef, biscuit, cheese, ale, brandy and water, bed at one. Earl Bruce in Queen's box ce soir.

JANUARY 6 ♦ Arose half past eight, breakfast half past nine, rehearsal at eleven, walked at half past one with Ellis from theatre to 2 Tavistock Row, Covent Garden, attended Drury Lane meeting, met on my way home Ellen Fitzpatrick & her sister in Endell Street. Dinner at four, roast mutton, potato, boiled plum pudding, brandy, biscuit, cheese, ale, port and sherry. Tea at six, theatre half past six, incl. Ellen, acted in one piece, home half past ten. Supped at eleven, cold roast mutton, biscuit, cheese, ale. Brandy and water and cake with Betsy. Bed at one.

JANUARY 7 ♦ Piece of Baddely's Twelfth Night cake from Drury Lane Theatre for Betsy and myself – lots of luck.

JANUARY 11 ♦ Rode at half past ten to Sackville Street, saw J.H. Parkinson about my teeth, then called upon my godson Charles Harley Savory in Regent Street. Rehearsal (Midsummer Night's Dream) at twelve.

JANUARY 12 ♦ In buss at half past eleven to Upper Southwark Street, saw Mat and her mother, took them brandy, sherry, cake (Robb, St Martin's Lane) and Twelfth Cake, Baddely's from D.L. Theatre, tasted both cakes & took with them cold brandy and water. Rehearsal of Hamlet at one.

JANUARY 26 ♦ Read to Betsy the Times report of the Royal Marriage, celebrated yesterday.

JANUARY 27 ♦ Wrote to order ale from Romford and clothes from Cutler. Rode to Parsons, Oxford Street, had my hair cut. Gossiped in Oxford Street with Same the Librarian, ordered new hat of Heath in Oxford Street, home to dinner at four.

FEBRUARY 5 ♦ Received Birthday presents from Betsy a new suit of clothes made by Cutler of St James's Street, and a new hat from Heath Oxford Street and also a new pair of cashmere gloves. Gave Betsy a new pair of walking shoes. Many happy returns of this day to us all.

FEBRUARY 10 ♦ This day Betsy and myself visited R.C. Dawson, 7 Queen Square, Westminster, met him and his 4 daughters with his sons George and Ambrose, also Mr Harper and Fanny Pritt. During our visit we saw the mortal remains of our dear cousin Annie Dawson, prepared for interment on Saturday next, God rest her soul.

FEBRUARY 13 ♦ Rode at 10 in mourning coach with Wm Dawson to Christ Church Broadway to hear funeral service at eleven, then to Brompton Cemetery, burial service by Mr Page. Back at one to Queen Square. Fowl, ham, bread, sherry, soda water. Theatre, home at three, dinner at four. Roast mutton, potato, biscuit, cheese, ale, brandy, port and sherry. Tea at six. Theatre half past six. Acted in one piece. Home half past ten, supped at eleven, cold mutton, cheese, biscuit, cheese, ale, brandy and water. Bed quarter before one.

MARCH 11 ♦ Broke my spectacles before breakfast, Betsy got them repaired for me in Tottenham Court Road before I went out.

MARCH 25 ♦ Rehearsal at eleven. Went with Ellen to Hyam's, Oxford Street, measured for new suit of clothes for Coake's new farce.

MARCH 27 ♦ Gave Betsy Illustrated News of this day with portrait of me as Bob Acres by Mayall, and memoir of Mark Lemon, lots of luck and God bless us all.

Curiously, John Harley was mistaken – in fact the illustration shows him as Tony Lumpkin, another of his famous roles.

APRIL 2 ♦ Betsy's birthday. Gave and received presents. Gave Betsy a pair of new walking shoes and received from her a pair of new elastic boots made by Thierry, Regent Street Quadrant, which I wore for the first time, this with a pair of new stockings. Lots of luck and God bless my dearest sister Betsy and myself.

APRIL 29 ♦ Gossiped today in Endell Street with Charles Dickens.

MAY 17 ♦ This is the anniversary of the burial of my beloved mother. Bumpers of sherry out of mother's glasses with Betsy, off silver salver, to the memory of our dear mother and our dear sister Mary.

MAY 20 ♦ Betsy bought pickles today in Soho Square and ordered new worked slippers (by Ellen) to be made for me at Hales, Charlotte Street, Bedford Square.

MAY 25 ♦ Betsy called today at 46 Gower Street & saw Mrs Armstrong and Mary. She also walked to Cribbs's Southampton Row to get her watch regulated. This day Betsy gave me for a Whitsuntide present a pair of slippers made by Hale, Charlotte Street, Bedford Square, the fronts worked for me by Ellen. Lots of luck and God bless us all.

JUNE 20 ♦ Had it pleased the Almighty to have spared to us our dear Mother she would this day have entered her 103rd year.

JULY 21 ♦ A public meeting in aid of the Dramatic College was held today at the Royal Princesses Theatre, Charles Kean in the chair.

AUGUST 5 ♦ Went at two o'clock today with Betsy to Kensill Green Cemetery and saw the stone placed over the remains of our dear sister Mary, being our second visit together to the spot since we first went there in September 1856 after the burial of our beloved sister Mary. Rode home half past three. Had wine out of mother's glasses and biscuit out of sister Mary's silver basket, to the memory of our beloved Mother and our beloved sister Mary. Dinner half past four. Roast beef, French beans, biscuit, cheese, brandy and water, port, sherry. Tea at seven.

On 20 August John Harley went on stage for the last time. He played Lancelot Gobbo, in The Merchant of Venice, *as he had so often done before, but collapsed in the wings after the performance with a paralytic stroke. His friends carried him home to 14 Upper Gower Street, where he died two days later. His last words are supposed to have been a quotation from* A Midsummer Night's Dream – *'I have an exposition of sleep come upon me'. He joined his relations at Kensal Green Cemetery on 28 August, and it emerged that despite his successful career and apparent prosperity he had died penniless. All his goods were sold to raise money for Betsy, including his collection of over 300 walking sticks and canes. What happened to poor Betsy is not known.*

ARTHUR PECK
Stonemason

Arthur Peck worked in the family stonemasonry business at 57 Fore Street, Hertford and was still living at home with his father when he started this diary in 1860 at the age of 21. He came from a large family. Several of his brothers and sisters had left home to work; some remained at home as he did. It is clear from the way he expresses himself that he had a good basic education, perhaps at the British School, and if his spelling and grammar are a little erratic, the meaning is clear enough. Not one to pour out his feelings, the entries relating to his long-running courtship of 'D.B.' are laconic but frequent. Their engagement passes without comment except for a neutral reference to an 'engaged ring' and a visit to the photographer's studio, clearly for a celebratory portrait. D.B. was almost certainly in domestic service, probably with one of the prominent local families, as she moved about from one great house to another. Panshanger Hall and Wrest Park belonged to the family of the Earls Cowper, Balls Park to the Marquis Townshend and Tolmers Park to the Mills family. The 'Hospital' at which Arthur and his brothers so often worked was the preparatory section of Christ's Hospital, a public school in Fore Street. Arthur's brother David, married to Patty, lived nearby at Watton at Stone, where he was the Poor Law relieving officer.

JANUARY 1 1860 ♦ Showery and mild. I went to the Wesleyan Chapel all day heard Mr Bartlett in the morning from the 9th chap. Isaiah 6th verse in the evening from the 37th chap. of Ezekiel 9th verse. D.B. was here to breakfast. She went to Chapel. I was at her house to tea. Mr and Mrs Errington came here at night. Mr Rose gave an address to the School. Fine night.

JANUARY 2 ♦ Very fine and mild. I was cutting letters all day in Church Yard. Aunt Sarah and Ben came here. D.B. went to C. Bailey's Cole Green. I, Joe and Ben

Messrs Gilbertson & Son   Xmas 1889

HEAD STONES · CHIMNEY PIECES · MONUMENTS

TOMBS, TABLETS, MONUMENTS

INSCRIPTIONS CUT & BLACKED.

Marble Stone Chimney Pieces in Variety

ESTABLISHED OVER 120 YEARS.

ARTHUR PECK,
SON OF THE LATE DAVID PECK.

Stone, Marble & Granite
MONUMENTAL WORKS.

FORE ST. & St JOHN'S Rd
HERTFORD.

Monumental Work executed & reinstated in the best manner.
ESTIMATES & DESIGNS FORWARDED ON APPLICATION.

1888			
Oct 26th & Nov 5th	Mason taking up paving getting out ground cutting hole through brick wall relaying paving etc at Mangrove. 1 hod mortar ¼ pk cement	4	
1889 March 11 & 12	Mason conveying to & from garden in Church Street, own old slate, cutting holes through ditto, preparing, fitting, & fixing same in greenhouse Church St. ½ pk cement etc.	11	6
Aug 23	Mason rubbing out snips & cleaning Marble Chimney-piece & hearth in morning room at Mangrove. Grit, sand, snake, etc.	8	6
		£ 1	4 0

ONE OF ARTHUR'S INVOICES

went to Popular Entertainment at Corn Exchange. Mr Y. Crawley read. Very fine night. Quarter Sessions, 12 prisoners.

JANUARY 3 ◆ Very showery and mild. We was at work at home. Joe drove Pris and Emma to Watton to keep house for David and Patty came home with him slept here. I and Ben went up Mangrove Lane with the dogs. The keeper came and warned us. Fine night and moonlight.

JANUARY 4 ◆ Very fine and mild. David and Patty went to London and back for £2 odd. Patty's uncle left. Father drove Aunt S and Ben to Watton and back. Mr Smithman came here ordered a stone to go to Ongar.

JANUARY 5 ◆ Very showery and cool. Joe drove David and Patty home and took David his round to Walham Aston and Bennington and brought Pris and Emma home here. Aunt Sarah went to Harlow. I and Joe went to Mr Laugher Bible Class. Very wet night. We had sprats for supper.

JANUARY 6 ◆ Showery and cold. Father was blacking letters all day. Pris and Emma went to Midday Prayer Meeting. I and Jim and Ben went to Ware Cemetery to fix Biscoe's head and feet stone. Mr Laugher came here and I went down to see D.B. mother.

JANUARY 7 ◆ Sharp frost and fine. Ben went to Harlow. We gave him Brisk our dog. Father went to meet David, I and Jim was fixing chimney pieces for N. Green at Hertford Heath. I went to Cole Green C. Bailey's for D.B. We sold 4 hens for 7/6d. I was very tired. Sharp frost at night and moonlight.

JANUARY 8 ◆ Sharp frost and fine. I went to Wesleyan Chapel all day heard Mr Laugher in the morning from the 10th chap. of John 16th and 17th verses in the evening from the 3rd chap. of Hosea 15th verse. I and D.B. went to Hertingfordbury for a walk. She went to Mrs Hickmans. I went to tea with her. I had a very bad head ache.

JANUARY 9 ◆ We was at work at home. We presented J. Hughes with a new bat, pads and gloves at his own house. 25 of us there. I and Joe came away between 10 and 11. I went down to D.B. C. Briden was helping her. Cold night.

JANUARY 10 ◆ We was at work at Hospital. I bought a Cochin China cock of Mr Keymer for 1s. I went down to D.B. C.B. was there and Liz M. I and D.B. went to Hertingfordbury. I felt very queer.

The Pecks were prone to constant minor ailments. A push is a boil, or pimple.

JANUARY 12 ◆ Pris was in bed all day sadly. Father was very queer with a cold. I had a little push up my nose very soar. We had a letter from Ann. I and Jim fixed

Travell's head and feet stone in Stanstead Church Yard new one. I went down to D.B. at night. She had a present from Mrs Mitchells, Tolmers, Mince pies &c &c. She wrote back to her.

JANUARY 13 ♦ We was at work at home. Tom Cook fell off the scaffold at Bengeo church, nearly 100 ft high.

JANUARY 14 ♦ T Cook better than expected. I and Jim at work at Hospital. Joe went to meet David. Joe had a letter from Ann. I paid B. Little £8 for Worsted cord trousers and waistcoat. I went down to D.B. at night. We both had a cold.

JANUARY 16 ♦ I was cutting letters. Pris went to help D.B. all day. I went down at night. Mr Errington read at the Popular Entertainment. I had a very bad cold. Father went to bed early queer.

JANUARY 17 ♦ I was cutting letters in Church Yard all day very cold. I, D.B. and Pris went to Teachers Meeting at Cowbridge. I was made Librarian.

Arthur was an active member of Cowbridge Independent Chapel.

JANUARY 18 ♦ I lost old Smoker our dog up Mangrove Lane. Father was bill making all day.

JANUARY 27 ♦ I and Jim fixed a flat chimney piece up Wells Field at Georges public house. Father, mother and Emma went to a Revival Meeting at Town Hall afternoon. I, Joe, Pris and Emma went at night – a very nice meeting.

FEBRUARY 1 ♦ Sharp frost and fine. I, Father, and Joe and Mr Shippin went rabbitt shooting at Howe Green killed 5. I was very tired.

FEBRUARY 3 ♦ Deep snow. I and Jim at work at Hospital. We lost a hen. I had a very bad cold.

FEBRUARY 4 ♦ I had a letter from D.B. at Tolmers. Pris sent Mrs Mitchell's sleeves to Tolmers. A little boy run over and killed up Castle St, named Wackett from Upper Green.

FEBRUARY 5 ♦ I wrote to D.B. at Tolmers. I had teeth ache. We had a fire in the parlour.

FEBRUARY 6 ♦ Snow storms very cold. I was painting head stones. D.B. came home from Tolmers. Had her likeness taken and came here to tea. I had teeth ache and was very cross.

FEBRUARY 7 ♦ I was cutting letters all day. I hurt my side raising a head stone. I went to Hertingfordbury for D.B.

FEBRUARY 8 ♦ I was painting head stones. I and Jim fixed a slab of marble in Mr Notcutt's shop for father. Cowbridge Teachers and Friends Annual Tea Meeting at Town Hall. I took ticketts 300 to tea. D.B. there. I went home with her.

FEBRUARY 10 ♦ I sold a hen to Arthur Jackson for 2s 6d.

FEBRUARY 11 ♦ Very sharp frost. Snowed nearly all day. Jim lost time. I was blacking letters all day. I went to Hertingfordbury with D.B. We had a rough walk.

FEBRUARY 14 ♦ I, Father and Joe went rabbitt shooting at Howe Green and ferretting with Mr Young killed 20 rabbitts. I, Joe and A. Wenham went down to Chapel arranging Library books till 10.

FEBRUARY 15 ♦ I and A. Wenham was making a catalogue of Books at Chapel till 10 o'clock.

FEBRUARY 16 ♦ I and Jim at work at Hospital. We set a hen on 12 eggs. I had a bad head ache. Green the Upholsterer failed.

FEBRUARY 17 ♦ Mother and Pris very sadly. D.B. came up here at night. I went down to her house at night, took her my Diary.

FEBRUARY 18 ♦ I was blacking letters all day. I was on the Jury a man died in the jail. Died a natural death. We went in the jail to see him.

FEBRUARY 20 ♦ Snow storm and cold. I was blacking letters. Father went down to Cole Green. Joe went to Ware for Brown. An accident occurred on Eastern Counties at Tottenham. Several killed.

FEBRUARY 21 ♦ I went down to D.B. her birthday, 21. I gave her a morocco basket.

FEBRUARY 26 ♦ I and D.B. went to Cowbridge Chapel all day. I gave books out of the Library for the first time. I went to D.B. to tea. We stayed at Prayer Meeting at night. I had a cold.

FEBRUARY 27 ♦ We was at work at home. A. Wenham came here. We was doing Library books. Mr Nichols died last night. Mr Inskipp died today with Diphthea.

FEBRUARY 29 ♦ Very fine and cool. A man drowned down by Gas House a barge mender.

MARCH 1 ♦ Jim not at work. I and Joe at work at home. We bought a dog of a Luton chap for 2s 6d. I went down to D.B. at night.

MARCH 2 ♦ Mr Inskip buried. We fetched Nicholls head and feet stone home. Jim went as bearer to Mr Inskip funeral.

MARCH 3 ♦ I finished working head stone with a scrowl. Father had a soar throat.

MARCH 4 ♦ Our dog got loose and we lost him. I had tea down at D.B. Mother very sadly.

MARCH 5 ♦ We was at work at home. D.B. went to Tolmers. Mother sadly.

MARCH 6 ♦ Mr Middlemas from Tolmers called here for a book for D.B. I had a cold. Emma queer and went to bed early.

MARCH 7 ♦ I sent D.B. a Fashion book to Tolmers by Butcher. I was making up Library book at night.

MARCH 30 ♦ We was working marble all day. DB came here to tea and supper I went home with her. Patty came here from Watton got a ride with J. Harris butcher. Got a very bad cold.

APRIL 2 ♦ I was painting head stones all day. Father was on the Jury at Sessions. Patty went home to Watton with Mr Parker the butcher. Club night at Dimsdale Arms I went paid up. Missionary Meeting at Wesleyan Chapel. Father, Mother and Emma went. Mother's birthday, 63.

APRIL 5 ♦ I and Joe was carting stone and pebbles from Cowbridge. We set a hen on 13 duck eggs and one on 13 hens eggs. Ann came home for a holiday from Malton. I went down to D.B.

APRIL 6, GOOD FRIDAY ♦ I went cricketing all day. Charles Whittaker came here to dinner. Father, Mother Ann and C. Whittaker went to Watton in a four wheel chaise left Ann there.

APRIL 7 ♦ Father and Pris went to meet David and Ann with a four wheel chaise. Ann had her portrait taken. I was very stiff.

APRIL 9 ♦ I and Father went rabbitt shooting at Howe Green killed 15. D.B. went to Mr Linghams at Cole Green. Mother had her portrait taken.

APRIL 10 ♦ Ann went off to Malton. Father went to London with her. We turned a live rabbitt in Laitham our lurcher caught and carried it home. We lost old Spot yesterday. I went and found him up Wall Fields.

APRIL 13 ♦ Mr Emerson a rider came here plaister Traveller. I and Joe went cricketing at night.

APRIL 14 ♦ We had a letter from Ann. Pris had a sick head ache.

APRIL 24 ♦ David came here Auditt day. Miss Baines the youngest married to Jones. I was putting a slate cistern together. I went down to D.B.

APRIL 25 ♦ We had a letter from Aunt Susan. We measured the street paving. I bought a doe rabbitt and 4 young ones for 4s. D.B. came up here. I went to Bengeo with her to Palmers. She sprained her knee.

APRIL 26 ♦ We had a hen come off with 11 chicks.

Sister-in-law Patty was expecting another baby.

APRIL 28 ♦ The nurse came from London for Patty. Joe drove her and David to Watton. Emma walked to Watton. Joe brought her and 2 children home.

APRIL 30 ♦ We were fixing slate cistern at Mrs Newmans Butchers. Jim sawing all day. The Militia came out. I went cricketing at night. I went home with D.B.

MAY 4 ♦ We was at work at home. I sold 2 hens for 4s 4d. I went cricketing at night.

MAY 9 ♦ I bought 10 pheasants eggs for 4s 6d. Rifle Dinner at Corn Exchange about 200 to dinner. I went cricketing at night. I had a very bad head ache.

MAY 10 ♦ My pheasant eggs turned out bad.

MAY 24 ♦ Very fine very hot. Municipal Election caused by the death of Mr Inskip. Frances got in beat Armstrong by 88.

MAY 25 ♦ Patty was confined had a fine girl.

JUNE 4 ♦ I was up half the night with teeth ache. I had teeth ache very bad all day.

JUNE 5 ♦ Father went to London. I was blacking letters all day. Little Arthur had his neck handkerchief stolen off his neck by a girl coming home from school. I had teeth ache.

JUNE 15 ♦ I had a push on my neck. I went cricketing at night and to Hertingfordbury for D.B. She was very sadly.

JUNE 16 ♦ I had one of Chamberlain's plaisters on my push. We had a letter from Ann.

JUNE 18 ♦ My push very soar. Pris went down to D.B. to help make mourning.

JUNE 21 ♦ My push very sore.

JUNE 22 ♦ I bought Smarts bird and cage gave it D.B. My push very painfull.

JUNE 23 ♦ The Rifles went to Hyde Park Review day. My push very bad.

JUNE 24 ♦ My push better.

JUNE 25 ♦ We sent Ann a post office order for 1s.

JULY 11 ♦ Very hot and fine. We were at work at home. The Assises commence. David and Emma came home from Watton. Father went cricketing in afternoon and got hit on the thumb.

JULY 12 ♦ I went in Court in the afternoon heard 3 men tried for Murder, shooting a keeper, got clear of it. Then charged for poaching. I went cricketing at night.

AUGUST 1 ♦ Very fine and hot. Hatfield Races great many went. We were at work at home. I and Joe went cricketing at night. D.B. came here.

AUGUST 7 ♦ We were laying paving and curb in Back St. Pris and Emma went to Watton. Odd Fellows Pic Nic in Lord Cowpers Park.

AUGUST 8 ♦ We were laying paving in Back St. Got wet through. D.B. went to Panshanger.

SEPTEMBER 18 ♦ Father was blacking letters. Father took out a County Court summons for Sheffield at Bengeo £50. I went down to D.B. had teeth ache.

SEPTEMBER 20 ♦ The Balls Park went to play the Hitchen and beat them.

SEPTEMBER 21 ♦ I was most mad with teeth ache.

OCTOBER 10 ♦ Very wet and very cold. I had teeth ache very bad & had one drawn by Dr Reilly high tooth.

OCTOBER 12 ♦ Had teeth ache very bad.

THE COURT AT NEWGATE PRISON

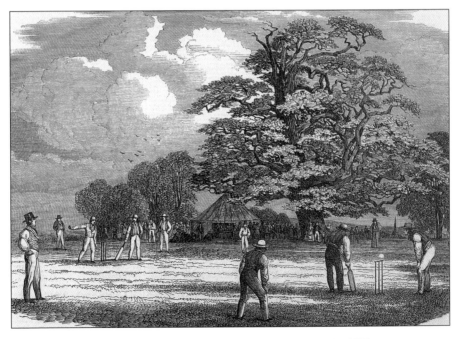

ARTHUR OFTEN MENTIONS HOW HE ENJOYED A GAME OF CRICKET

OCTOBER 13 ♦ Emma had teeth ache. I had a cold.

OCTOBER 16 ♦ Very wet and cold. I was working marble all day. D.B. went to Panshanger. We had a letter from Ann. I had a bad cold indeed had diareah very bad.

NOVEMBER 28 ♦ Father and Mother went to Harlow Town Fair. I and Joe were laying curb opposite Shippen's. I was very tired, went to Panshanger for D.B. went in the dining room saw the dinner service. Splendid plate. She had a bad cold.

NOVEMBER 30 ♦ I was blacking letters all day till 8 o'clock. David walked here and home again about that wretched bill to see Mr Sworder. I killed 2 young cocks. Emma went to Ragged School at night to hear Mr Harrison.

DECEMBER 2 ♦ My birthday 22. We went to Cowbridge all day heard Mr Pannicott for the first time settled amongst us liked him very much in the morning. We stayed to Prayer Meeting after the evening service. I had tea at D.B.

DECEMBER 3 ♦ I had a letter from Ann a Birthday present a shoe lace.

DECEMBER 8 ♦ David went to London about that wretched bill. Father and Mother's Wedding Day been married 36 years. Emma's birthday 26 years.

DECEMBER 10 ♦ Joe went to meet David. He went to London about that wretched bill. They took £20 off. He walked home to Watton from here at night.

DECEMBER 13 ♦ We bought a ferrett for 4s. D.B. finished at Ginns. I went home with her. I had a bad head ache.

DECEMBER 17 ♦ Showery and cold. Snow storms. Mother in bed nearly all day. Very queer. Father went to Ware horse back. I and Joe ran up in Pike Cousin's Gravel pit caught a rat for the ferret. Mother very sadly.

DECEMBER 18 ♦ I and Joe and G. Castle went ferretting up Sandy Lane in the afternoon caught nothing. Emma went to Miss Bourchier's working class. I went down to see D.B. mother at night. Mother very queer. 9 degrees of frost at night.

DECEMBER 25 ♦ Very fine sharp frost. The glass down below zero. Joe had a fly went to Watton brought David, Patty and kids here. I, Joe and David went shooting all afternoon on Townshend's Canal. I was very stiff and tired. Our gas mantle frozen, I thawed it with hot water.

DECEMBER 26 ♦ I and Joe went rabbitting at Howe Green caught 5 rabbitts, Fred Collins won a bottle of Port for I in lottery. I and Joe got a ride home from Burkhamsted Nunn cart. Another man that rode with us drunk rolled out cut his chin.

DECEMBER 28 ♦ Ann came home from Malton a fortnight's holiday.

JANUARY 4 1861 ♦ I and Joe walked to Howe Green ferritting rabbits. Mr Young gave us 3. We got a ride home. Just in time, Father had let our gas mantle get on fire nearly [burned? – word omitted] the shop. I put it out. D.B. came up here. I went home with her. Very tired, had teeth ache.

JANUARY 7 ♦ Dr J Evans' horse run away broke the chaise in Fore St.

JANUARY 8 ♦ I and Joe went skating. I sold a pair of skates for 4s. We bought old Smoker our dog back for 4 hens and 1/6d. We had a hen die. I went to Cole Green for D.B. got home at 11. Had a jolly row with the grumbling old man. He threatened to lock me out. We played at cricket on the ice. A great many people there.

JANUARY 9 ♦ I did not speak to Father all day. I and Joe went skating.

FEBRUARY 21 ♦ I went down to D.B. at night. Her birthday 22. She gave me a pair of slippers her own working.

FEBRUARY 24 ♦ I had tea at D.B. She sobbed bitterly at night, felt her sins very great.

Arthur left home to find another job, perhaps as a result of the recent row with his father. His rather incoherent entry for 25 February may reflect his upset state of mind.

FEBRUARY 25 ♦ I left home, walked to Stratford from Stort. to Dunmow 20 cold miles saw Jim Nicoll. I was on the road saw J Nicoll at Stortford. I went down to D.B. before I started. I was very tired only spent 5 ½ all day. Slept at the Royal Oak Dunmow got there at ½ past 9. Did not sleep well at all. Cold night.

FEBRUARY 26 ♦ I paid 9d for bed and breakfast. I walked from Dunmow to Braintree 9 miles and from Braintree to Chelmsford 12 miles called in 2 yard at B got a ride 2 miles. I called at Wray's yard at Chelms. no go a young man named Herbert gave me 3d. I called at Mr Hardy yard saw Mr H he took me in gave me bread and meat and beer. I bought a beef steak and Bread at Braintree spend 1s all day. Mr H paid my lodging at the Friars Inn. Another tramp slept in same room.

FEBRUARY 28 ♦ I was at work in yard all day. Very fine day. I went for a walk round the Town at night.

MARCH 1 ♦ I was at work in the yard. I saw F. Briden and Mr Archer in the market. I wrote to Mother and D.B.

MARCH 2 ♦ Mr H paid me 15s 3 days ¾. I shifted my lodging to private lodging to Mr Gentry, Fruiterer &c, High St.

MARCH 3, SUNDAY ♦ I wrote home and to D.B. Mrs Gentry, Father, Mother and sister named Brown came here to dinner and tea. Mr B birthday. They gave me some apple pie, oranges and plum cake. I went to Baddow Road Chapel at night. I had all my working things on.

MARCH 5 ♦ The Judge came in for Assises. We were at work in yard. Fine night.

MARCH 6 ♦ I had a letter from D.B. Mother, David and Joe. I and Mr Gentry went

ARTHUR'S FIANCÉE, D.B., WAS ALMOST CERTAINLY IN DOMESTIC SERVICE

to service at Wesleyan Chapel at night, heard Mr Swallow. Mr Gentry read and preached.

MARCH 8 ♦ I had a bad cold and head ache.

MARCH 10 ♦ I saw a man swim and save a cow from drowning. I went to Baddow Road chapel at night in Mr G greatcoat.

MARCH 11 ♦ Mr H was out all day. We were at work in yard. Trade very bad. I had a fearful cold.

MARCH 13 ♦ I had a sore throat. I had my box come.

MARCH 17 ♦ I went to a fire, a straw stack at Barnses Farm. They took a man on suspicion. 2 engines came.

MARCH 23 ♦ I had a letter from Joe and Mother, Father wanted me home.

MARCH 28 ♦ Showery and cold. I left off at dinner time went home by calf cart walked from Eastwick 8 o'clock to St Margarets got there soon after 9 saw the train go by could not get a ticket had a row with Mr Williams the Station Master, went in his house had a pipe &c stayed for last train got home just 1 o'clock. All in bed. I was very tired.

MARCH 29, GOOD FRIDAY ♦ I went down to D.B. in the morning. Father and Mother went to Watton after dinner, I went down to D.B. after dinner. Jim and I back at work all day. I felt rather queer.

The next entry is written upside down. Mr Marks was a local silversmith and jeweller.

MARCH 30 ♦ D.B. and Pris went to Mr Marks. D.B. had an engaged ring 13s.

APRIL 1 ♦ I went down to D.B. at night. She was very queer indeed.

APRIL 2 ♦ D.B. queer. Father fell off a railway truck hurt his side very much had Dr Reilly. I and D.B. went to Mr Forscutts had our portraits taken 2 double ones 1 single one of myself. D.B. had hers in a case. 10/6d all together. Joe bought my share of fowls 10s. I came back to Chelmsford. D.B. at our house to dinner. Mother's birthday, 64 years old. It cost me 5s 11d to come back.

APRIL 3 ♦ I went to work first thing. Gentry and his Wife fell out. I had a bad cold. I wrote to D.B. and Mother.

APRIL 13 ♦ Gentry gave his wife a black eye, made her ill.

APRIL 15 ♦ I was at work in town and yard. Hardy at work very bad tempered with me.

APRIL 23 ♦ I and Frank finished at old Bank. Mr H came and swore at us. All right in a few minutes. I and Gentry had an argument about Wife beating, I get his monky.

MAY 6 ♦ Mr Loveday was buried the grave not large enough. Gentry helped to carry.

MAY 8 ♦ Fine and cool. Gentry went out no one knew where. I went to Mrs Loveday with Tom. Engaged lodgings. Gentry did not come home. Mrs Brown came up to sleep with Mrs G.

MAY 9 ♦ Gentry came home, been to Braintree Fair, went to London and back. I gave notice to leave them.

MAY 10 ♦ I went for a walk with T. Loveday. They had Gentry before the Deacons.

MAY 13 ♦ I came to lodge with Mrs Loveday. Fair day. Pretty good fair.

JUNE 5 ♦ Very fine and hot. A great many went to Races. I was cutting letters in St John's churchyard all day. A house was broken into close bye, by 2 men, they got away. I, W. Markeham and W. Copsey took a walk on the race course at night, coming home Hardy passed us, drunk driving furiously. He upset after he got past. We put him in the cart. I drove him home, but his forehead very much [injured? – word omitted]. Mrs Loveday went to sit up with him all night.

JUNE 6 ♦ Fine and cool. I was cutting letters. Mr H very queer. I had a bad head ache.

JUNE 7 ♦ We were at work in yard. Mr H very queer in bed all day. Mr Mayson, the Registrar of Births and Deaths, got killed coming home from the races on the buss going in the gateway at the Bell Inn. Hit his head, a van upset too, 15 in a pond.

JUNE 11 ♦ We were at work at Barnses Mill. I went in to see Mr H., had some beer, a little better, downstairs. I went gardening at night for Mrs L. I was very tired indeed. Felt weak in the loins.

JUNE 14 ♦ I wrote to D.B. wishing her to come down here. Sent her a half sov.

JUNE 15 ♦ Very hot and fine. I was at work at seven. A boy drowned whilst bathing named Maypole. I went bathing at night, had a chat with Mr Wray. He went to see Mr H about my working for him.

JUNE 16 ♦ My hair oil bottle broke in my hand, on my trousers etc.

JUNE 26 ♦ Fine and hot. Mr H went out. I went up to W. Markham's. We went to Emidy's Circus. Very good indeed. I had a bad cold. Mrs L sat up for me nearly 11. She was very cross indeed, so was I.

JUNE 27 ♦ I had a letter from mother wishing me to come home.

JUNE 28 ♦ We were at work in yard. I came home by calf cart young T Archer drove, to Eastwick, walked from dº to St Margarets very tired. Went home with D.B.

JUNE 29 ♦ I felt very queer. I bought trousers, waistcoat, coat and caps at Neals, £1.16s.

JULY 9 ♦ I went down to D.B. had a regular tiff. She came up here after dinner. Had a letter from Hardy wanting me back. I went cricketing and bathing at night.

JULY 10 ♦ I went back to Chelmsford the Feate on Springfield lawn. I left Hardy because he would not give me more than 4s per day.

JULY 11 ♦ I came home from Chelmsford went about London a great deal, went to Mr Mannings (Sculptors) could not see him. Very tired, felt queer.

Back in Hertford again, Arthur resumed his usual activities.

DECEMBER 3 ♦ Very sharp frost and fine. We were at work at home. D.B. here all day. I had a fearful cold, headache and tooth ache. Mother had a cold. Emma went to Watton and back. I went home with D.B. was very queer.

MAY 30 1862 ♦ Showery and hot. Harpenden races. I and Jim at work at Judds. I and Jim at work at Hospital all day. Father went to meet David. We had a letter from Pris at Margate. I went cricketing at night and for a walk with D.B. Very fine night, and hot.

OCTOBER 11 ♦ Thundered and lightened. We were at work at home. My Rabbitt had 5 young ones, I sold 2 young rabbitts for 1s. Joe went to Watton with mare, brought Patty, Pris and Arthur, Lill and Emily here. We turned the mare and pony down Laitham. I had a painfull head ache. I went down to D.B. at night.

DECEMBER 21 ♦ Joe's birthday 22. Joe fetched the pony from Mead's, Father queer, in all day. I and D.B. went to Wesleyan Chapel in the morning, heard Mr Holmes.

MARCH 19 ♦ I and Jim at work at Hospital and at home. Father went to London. We had a letter from dear Ann. Pris went to tea at Miss Quants at Hospital. D.B. came up here, I went home with her. My cough very troublesome.

OCTOBER 30 ♦ A tremendous wet day and cold. We were at work at home. Pris at Dears all day. I and Joe went to the Chess Club at night. I had a cold.

OCTOBER 31 ♦ I had a letter from D.B. at Wrest Park. I was very tired.

DECEMBER 31 ♦ Fine and cold. We were at work at home. Father took out a summons for Berington and Topham. Topham and Mr Jones from the College came here. D.B. at Austins. We went to Watch Night at Gt Church heard Mr Birch preach. Pris went to Wesleyan Chapel. I had a cold. Very wet night indeed and very cold snowed and rained. D.B. slept here. We came to bed just after one.

END OF THE YEAR 1863

Arthur Peck's single bid for freedom from the family business – when he left home and took a job in Chelmsford – only lasted about four months. He does not spell out his reasons for leaving or returning, but the whole episode seems to have been triggered by the 'jolly row with the grumbling old man'. His trip to London to try and find work with Samuel Manning, the sculptor, surely indicates some yearning for a different life, but he soon returned to the family fold and resumed the old routine. His interest in local deaths may indicate genuine concern – or perhaps a professional interest in the forthcoming need for monumental masonry.

JOSEPH HÉKÉKYAN BEY
Archaeologist

Joseph Hékékyan Bey was a distinguished administrator and archaeologist of Armenian origin, working in the service of the Khedive of Egypt. In his youth he had studied in London. In this diary he records his return there in middle age – mainly on government business, to arrange for the publication of his scholarly book, A Treatise on the Chronology of Siriadic Monuments, *which appeared in print the following year. He also made time for pleasure, looking up old friends and bringing with him his wife and son on their first visit to England. Hékékyan presents an affectionate, outsider's view of London and English ways, with a keen eye for social nuances.*

JULY 7 1862, MONDAY ♦ Left Paris at 9.05 a.m. and reached London, the Victoria Station at 8.45 in the evening and put up in the Grosvenor Hotel.

JULY 8 ♦ Visited my good old friend Mr Briggs at Clarence House, East Sheen near Mortlake. At 86 he is still young, possessing all his mental faculties as at 43. Mrs Briggs and her maiden sister Miss Larking appear older than they should do. Mr & Mrs B entertained me at the Crystal Palace. Returned to G. Hotel by the midnight train.

JULY 9 ♦ Visited my good old friend Mr Collard in 22 Upper Hamilton Terrace, St John's Wood. He is quite gray, but as good and as hearty as ever. He and Mrs Collard drove me out into the parks.

JULY 13 ♦ I made this a day of rest in every sense. In the evening I dined with Mr Collard and met Mr and Mrs Benson at his hospitable table.

JULY 14 ♦ Saw the interesting exhibition of Madame Tussaud. The Adelphi.

His wife and son joined him from Paris, and they soon moved into private lodgings.

JULY 18 ♦ The Grosvenor was full, and after going the round of several hotels which were all full on account of their intrinsic worth in comfort and moderate charges

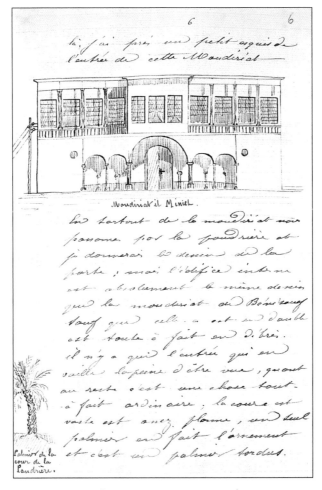

A SKETCH IN JOSEPH'S DIARY SHOWING A GOVERNOR'S HEADQUARTERS

ARABIC SCRIPT IN JOSEPH'S DIARY. JOSEPH SPOKE ENGLISH, FRENCH AND ARABIC

we found the Queen's Hotel in Cork Street in which we found plenty of room, I suppose from the comparative low scale of its material resources and exorbitant charges. While I reposed I sent my wife and son to be driven in a hired carriage in the parks and the principal streets.

JULY 19 ♦ After breakfast we drove down to our lodgings. My wife was pleased with them, humble as they are. They are clean, and the mistress of the house is, I am sure, a good lady. I could trust my son to her care. From the lodgings to the Great Exhibition it is a quarter of an hour's slow walk. We dined in the house – a roast joint of lamb with mint sauce and a dish of fresh peas. A currant tart. Cheese. The bread was found to be excellent. I ordered a pint and a half of table beer which they here call porter. The water is not bad, though for us water-drinkers we could have wished it to be lighter and sweeter. But we cannot be fair judges because we have been accustomed to the delicious Nile.

JULY 20 ♦ We found our bed rather too narrow for a couple. I shall order a moveable bed which may be put up and look like a chest of drawers in the day time. Heard Rd. Molineux preach in the church in Sumner Place near the Exhibition.

JULY 23 ♦ I purchased in Charing Cross a good map of London and three volumes of guides on England, Scotland and Ireland and a portfolio for writing paper, the bill amounting to 36s.

JULY 27, SUNDAY ♦ We received an invitation to go and pass the Sunday at Mr and Mrs Collard's. But unfortunately I had accepted an engagement to dine with Mrs Tuck and her family at Camden Town. On the whole we had a fine day. After Mass, which we heard at an Oratorio near the Kensington Museum, we visited Mr and Mrs Brunton. Afterwards we had a fine hazy view of London from the top of Primrose Hill. And at 4 we went to Mr Brown, where Mrs Tuck is living. Mr Brown keeps a chop house, and as the servants were all out on account of it being Sunday, he and his wife had to do every thing. We sat nine at table. I never was more happy in my life. There was as much good sense, cleanliness, order and female beauty as I have seen anywhere else, minus the affectation of learning and breeding. My wife, who is accustomed to the refinements of oriental courts, saw nothing improper or disagreeable in the society of these good people. In my estimation the distinctions made by Englishmen are as absurd as many of ours.

JULY 31 ♦ I went with my wife to make a morning call on Mr Murray at Claridge's Hotel. On the invitation of the servant who went up to announce our names, we followed him up to the third storey and had approached close to Mr

Murray's door, when I saw his head and heard him say to the servant "I am really very sorry, and regret that I cannot see them – for I must be in time for the train". I cared little for myself, but felt for my wife, it being probably the first time I had brought her to such a pass.

AUGUST 2 ♦ Spent 7 hours in the Exhibition. In the evening we dined out – having, as my wife desired, an oyster and fish kind of dinner, of which she is fond, and afterwards took her to the little theatre in the Haymarket. In the theatre it was oppressively warm and disagreeable. Lord Dundreary and Our American Cousin are well devised and well acted. The ballet of the Contrabandista pleased my wife.

AUGUST 25 ♦ Breakfasted early, and an excursion to the Crystal Palace took us the whole day. There was a poultry show and some of the cocks crowed like camels. Our Egyptian pigeons and turkeys are much finer than the best English. There was excellent music and above all a beautiful sunshine and clear atmosphere.

Like many visitors before and since, Joseph Hékékyan found a long visit to the British Museum tiring.

AUGUST 27, WEDNESDAY ♦ I sent my wife and son with Mrs Luce to see the Zoological Gardens and to make purchases of plated candlesticks and clothing for her. I rode to the Soane Museum to see Mr Bonomi. He told me he was engaged. I consequently proceeded alone to the British Museum. I was much struck with the Myrinan and Babylonian collections. The Museum is very extensive and the mere going over it knocked me up. After some refreshment I proceeded on foot to the Athenaeum and passed four hours reading the papers, looking over maps and peeping into books. I took a cup of coffee there, it was so strong that it made me squeamish. Returned home to dinner in an Omnibus.

He was not impressed by a performance at John Harley's old theatre, the Princess's.

SEPTEMBER 1 ♦ Now that I know the world nothing in the way of historical acting pleases me. Keane is no more Henry the Eighth than my wax light. The figure is good. When Buckingham was getting led to execution, he talked as if he was going to dine out with his mistress, and not a man or woman in the crowd showed any symptoms of sorrow.

SEPTEMBER 3 ♦ Dined in Regent Street. As I was returning to the club it commenced to rain, and like many others – men and women – I took shelter under a portico where there was a crowd. In the club I found that my purse, which I carried in my left waistcoat pocket, was missing. It contained about six guineas in gold and silver, some penny stamps and cartes de visite. I must have been robbed in the crowd under the portico. It is well I did not lose my watch also, which was in the other pocket.

SEPTEMBER 4 ♦ I bought a new purse, penny envelopes – and replenished it with my cards – and changed a £5 note. I passed an unpleasant night at the idea that I had been so careless. And if the cash in it had been all I possessed …

The 'Exhibition' visited by the Hékékyans was the International Exhibition of 1862, held on the site of the present Natural History Museum. Less of a draw than the Great Exhibition of 1851, it nevertheless attracted many visitors. Joseph and his wife also went to the Crystal Palace, the building in which the 1851 Exhibition had been staged, now re-erected in South London. It is interesting to note their visit to the Princess's Theatre, where John Harley had been such a stalwart performer a few years previously. Hékékyan does not give us his opinion of Richard Molineux, the famous preacher who had rather disappointed the Wyons in 1853.

AMY PEARCE
Young lady

Amy Pearce lived in Stroud, Gloucestershire, near George Pegler's family, with her parents and five sisters. Her only brother, Hugh, had recently left home in disgrace, and was suffering an alarming fall down the social scale. The Pearces were a middle-class family in comfortable circumstances, but Amy is beset by anxiety. Keeping a diary allowed her to confide her feelings in private, though she sometimes worried that others might read it. Since she is cautious about how much she writes down, it is hard for us to decide how many of her problems are the result of adolescent self-dramatization, and how many are due to external events not fully explained here. Either way, Amy, aged 20 as the diary opens, was frequently in a tense emotional state. The diary begins cheerfully enough, first on the subject of her clothes, then a Sunday School treat at a local farm.

JUNE 5 1873, FERN ROCK HOUSE, STROUD ♦ I mean to write in this book regularly once or twice a week. I have quite got out of the way of keeping a diary lately, it takes so much time. I really have none to spare just now. What with the children's lessons, the dress-making, practising reading, & going out, I scarcely ever have an idle moment, & I am very glad of it. I want my life to be a busy active industrious one. How much happier people are who have plenty to do. We have taken lately to making all our dresses and jackets at home, & this summer we have trimmed our own bonnets and hats. I want to write down here what I am going to wear, so that in after years I can see whether my taste has altered. My best dress is a soft drabby grey trimmed with satin to match, a long plain skirt & pretty polonaise. Then I have a circular cape of black cashmere trimmed with black silk and yarn lace, & a straw bonnet trimmed with black velvet white ribbon & a tip of ostrich feathers. I am going to have two white muslins for every day & I have a black and white silk & a pretty golden grey shot silk. My every day hat is a turn down black and white straw trimmed with

AMY CAME FROM A MIDDLE-CLASS FAMILY
OF COMFORTABLE CIRCUMSTANCES

COUSIN HENRY, WHOM AMY MARRIED
AFTER MUCH DELIBERATION IN 1886

AMY'S DIARY

black velvet ribbon. It is the fashion to wear one's hat at the back of the head, but I cannot bear it, it looks so fast.

I want to write something now about Whit Monday. We had such a long, tiring day. Cari & I walked out to Pitchcombe Farm, met about six of the other teachers, & cut up bread & butter & cakes nearly the whole morning. Then we had luncheon which Mr Freddy Winterbotham had provided for us, & then cut up again until about half past three, when the school children arrived in great waggons. After they had had tea, all the teachers & friends had theirs on the lawn & the rest of the evening the people walked about & the teachers helped to amuse the children. Doll ran about so much that she overdid herself & had to rest all the evening on a sofa. Mrs Weedon very kindly kept her all night at Pitchcombe.

The arrival of a new minister at the Independent chapel caused a stir. Amy and her sisters took a great fancy to him.

JULY 7, MONDAY ♦ I quite meant to have written in my diary yesterday, but it was such a very happy day that I did not feel inclined to do anything but enjoy it to the uttermost. Our new minister Mr Park preached his first sermons in Bedford Street chapel yesterday. They were so beautiful we were all more than satisfied with them, he spoke so nicely of his coming amongst us, & asked us to extend to him the same kindness & consideration we had always shown to Mr Wheeler. He said what a burden he felt it having to follow in Mr Wheeler's steps & then at the communion he made a most beautiful & appropriate address. It is indescribably pleasant to have really settled a minister, some one to look to & go to if we want help. I only pray that we may not think more of the messenger than of the message.

JULY 8 ♦ I broke off suddenly in my entry yesterday & as I have a great deal to note down I will make this a sort of continuation. Mr Park is coming to lodge just opposite us at Mrs Bidmead's. It will be nice & it will be nasty. We have heard nothing at all of dear Hugh but we have come to the conclusion that he went away intentionally. I feel sure, perfectly sure, that he is alright. I know that God knows just where he is, & I mean by God's help never to miss a morning or an evening without praying for him, if I leave everything else. He is a good deal in debt & Papa says he cannot and will not pay his bills. They are not anything very dreadful. I think 100 or 150 pounds would certainly cover them. Our three little ones are going to be baptised & join the church, and it is sweet &

beautiful to think that they are Christians. Aggie is very young but I believe she quite understands what she is doing. Emily is 14, Fanny 12 & Agnes eleven. Cari is going to Croydon on Friday to stay with the Whitings & then to London. It is her first visit alone. I wanted to go somewhere myself dreadfully a short time ago, but somehow I have felt more settled lately & I feel perfectly content to stay here now, the garden is so exquisitely lovely, such roses & lilies, geraniums, sweet peas, mignonette, fuschias & every kind of flower. I think I almost worship flowers.

JULY 22 ♦ As usual I make all kinds of resolutions & fail to keep them. I am feeling so wretched, so miserable, we heard today something dreadful, something I cannot & will not believe. Oh I pray God it may not be true, it is enough almost to shake one's confidence in God, in heaven, in everything. Dear Mr Chapman. It is about him, but I cannot say what it is. I do not, I will not believe it. It makes me so wretched. I feel I want to die. Is there no good really in the world? It seems to me as though every one I ever looked to as being upright, godly men was being taken away from me and I feel inclined to think that there is not a good man living. I am so miserable. My darling brother too, his sin is a light one compared with others. He has not written yet and we are still in complete ignorance as to where he is.

Mr Chapman was the Congregational minister.

JULY 26 ♦ I want to make a tiny entry in my diary. I do not know what for, but sometimes I have a feeling that I want to write & if I have time to, it does me good. I am afraid I am getting back into my old stupid unsettled way of thinking. I can't think what it is that makes me have these idiotic fits, but I cannot help it. I long for some change in my life. I want to be better. Why, why is my life such a useless one? I must do something. I will go and see the world.

SEPTEMBER 7 ♦ I have taken a very bad cold, playing croquet too late, so the consequence is I am debarred from going out today & have time to write in my diary. My life seems crowded up with all sorts of things, work and play. I am only afraid of crowding out Jesus. We all like our new minister as much as ever. He is very fond of croquet & when it was warm we often had games with him but I suppose croquet is almost over for this summer.

Amy and her sisters had taken a great liking to Mr Park, and were shocked when he brought his new bride to Stroud, not having mentioned his engagement to his congregation.

A VICTORIAN FAMILY IN THE GARDEN. AMY ADORED 'EXQUISITELY LOVELY' ROSES AND LILIES

SEPTEMBER 13 ♦ I cannot write here half of what I want to for fear of its being seen. It seems to me as though I had suddenly gone out of beautiful sunshine into a great black cloud. I have asked God to help, I have tried to cast it on him.

SEPTEMBER 18 ♦ The Sunday morning after I wrote that last entry I was feeling just as wretched & I could not help crying, & then C asked me what was the matter, & then she gave me the best piece of advice I have had for a long long time. She told me not to try not to care, and not to try to care, but just to give myself right up to Jesus. Since then I have felt better.

SEPTEMBER 22 ♦ Today at dinner time by the afternoon post we heard tidings of our dear brother. He has been in England again. Cousin Charlie saw him in London, & he told him he had been to Canada & was trying to earn money to pay all his creditors. Hugh sent us his best love & has promised to write to Uncle Tom occasionally to let him know where he is, so we shall hear now and then of his welfare.

SEPTEMBER 29 ♦ Poor Hugh has turned up at last. He is in London and has written in great distress. He says he has no money, clothes or lodging. What will become of Hugh I am sure I cannot tell. I am weary & tired & sick & I do not know what I want, or what is the matter with me.

OCTOBER 5 ♦ We heard from Hugh yesterday. He is still in London, but intends going to sea in a steamer, the Delta, bound for China. It is the only thing left for him to do, he is to go as a purser or steward, wretched enough. He has seen lately someone who wants me to be his wife still, & recommends me to think well over it & not refuse hastily as he is sure he would make a good husband. But I cannot. It is no use. I feel as if I wanted someone – well, I don't know exactly what I mean, but at any rate a dissenter, someone I could respect very much.

DECEMBER 21 ♦ Last Monday week Mama went to London to see Hugh. He has just started in one of the great troop ships carrying soldiers and provisions to the Ashantee war. Poor boy, he went as third steward, he was to have been made under-steward but one day while the ship was at Woolwich the officers gave a dinner, & Hugh was waiting table. One of the gentlemen made room for Hugh to sit down at table, thinking he was a guest, & Hugh thinks the captain was vexed because next day he put him down lower. Poor Hugh, his work will be just that of a scullery maid, & it is all through his own folly, he might be living here now, with every comfort of life. Cousin Charlie told Mamma that the real cause of his leaving Stroud was on account of his engagement to Miss Lane, he did not want to marry her & did not know how to get out of the scrape. He called it a violent flirtation, but I think it was absolute wickedness & cruelty, both to us & the poor girl. He says the sea life agrees with him, & perhaps he may be better after all, but oh what miseries he has to encounter. God preserve him. Mamma soon returned from London, the fog was so awful that she could not move about at all without risking her life. They say there had never been such a fog since 1805 & the accidents that took place were dreadful.

APRIL 12 1874 ♦ Hugh has returned from the Gold Coast & is looking out for some other employment. He is probably going to Australia. He has had a terribly rough journey, I don't mean rough weather, but rough work, poor fellow.

JULY 17 ♦ Since my last entry we, C & I, have been on such a long eventful visit to Devon. I am not at all prepared to say what happened there more than that I suppose the event will change the whole current of my life. It was a charming visit in one way, & yet we had a great many vexations & trials & I feel oh so sobered down, so old, people tell me I am looking careworn & altogether changed but things cannot happen to one without their making a difference.

AUGUST 16 ♦ I have as usual some sorrow always on hand. I have now just broken off my first engagement. It is not what one can write in girlish diaries about, but I wanted just to note it down. We, my dear cousin & I, were engaged first at Quay Cottage but since then I have not felt quite happy & yesterday (he came here last Friday) I begged him to let me off, but oh I am very unhappy.

SEPTEMBER 21 ♦ Today it is Fanny's birthday, she is 14. We are all getting so old that I really begin to feel quite alarmed, however as Carrie & I are both engaged I suppose it does not much matter, for I am engaged again. I could not be happy either when it was broken off, & now God grant that I may be very happy indeed. The cousins have been staying here, Pro & Henry, Pro for a month, Henry not quite so long. He my dear cousin has given me a lovely gold chain & brooch & I am to have my ring shortly. Many people have congratulated me most kindly though I fancy they all think Cousin Henry is too old for me.

MARCH 12 1875 ♦ Oh what a space, I don't believe I have such another in all my diary. Well, one great fact is that I am again unengaged. I do not like to think of it or write about it. I could not be happy & so after worrying and worrying I got bad & then I broke off my engagement. Now I am happier again & I do trust that I shall never be engaged again unless it is to someone who is really, really Christian, & one whom I can love with all my heart & soul. Henry has gone to India. I still have his chain & brooch until his return, but I am perfectly decided in my own mind. Some people say there are better things in store for me, but I don't know, at any rate I know I want better things very very sadly.

Amy's father, a cloth manufacturer, died at about this time, leaving the family in severe financial difficulty. Amy and her sister Emily went to London, to train as kindergarten teachers at the new Froebel college. Eventually they set up their own school. After 10 years, cousin Henry came home from India, where he had had a distinguished career as a doctor. He had written to Amy throughout this period, and she finally agreed to marry him in 1886 when she was 33 and he was nearly 60. They had two children, Henry and Amy. Young Amy later wrote that her mother had not been in love with her father, but married in the hope that Henry could bring the family some financial comfort. He died in 1908.

THE PEARCE FAMILY. AMY IS SEATED FAR RIGHT

THE DONALDSONS
Parents

Andrew Donaldson and his wife Agnes started a joint diary as soon as they married in June 1872, and continued it until their deaths. Andrew was an artist, specializing in the historical and genre paintings that Victorians so admired, and in landscapes. He exhibited at the Royal Academy and must have made a good income. They lived in London, at 10 Argyll Road, Kensington, with their five children and servants. In 1880 they decided to spend the winter in Rome, where Andrew had studied in the 1860s, and they set off en famille *on the tiring and difficult journey, with their nurse Bessie to help. With stops in Paris and Turin on the way out and Florence and Venice on the way back, they were away for seven months altogether. Their diary, with Andrew's delightful marginal illustrations, tells the story in full.*

Journey to Rome 1880.

NOVEMBER 1, ALL SAINTS DAY [ANDREW WRITES] ♦ We (A.B.D., A.E.D., Mary, Clement, Leonard & Dora, Phoebe and Bessie nurse) left London on the propitious feast of All Saints. A nice Omnibus took us to the Station and Mr Turning and Edith went with us to see the last of us. I had the previous Saturday sent the greater part of the luggage to the Station, thus saving time and trouble for the early start of 6.30 from Newburgh House. The guard kindly put the large party into a saloon carriage and the children greatly enjoyed the liberty the unusual space gave them. The sea looked smooth when we got to Folkestone, but did not prove altogether so as we proceeded on our voyage. I deposited the family in the deck-cabin and kept above myself. None were very bad, though the younger children were sick. We had sufficient time at Boulogne to get soup and to settle ourselves into a carriage, which we luckily again were allowed to have to ourselves. The children were amused at the strange appearance of things and people and Dora asked if the gens d'armes

ANDREW SKETCHED THROUGHOUT HIS DIARY

THE DONALDSONS WERE DELIGHTED BY VENICE

were "real men" or " 'tend men" (evidently thinking of Madame Tussaud). The journey to Paris was accomplished and the custom-house gone through without trouble – and we were glad to get our meals and go to bed at the Hotel du Nord.

NOVEMBER 2, TUESDAY ♦ The next morning was a lovely one. I took a short walk before breakfast and afterwards went with Mary, Clement and Leonard for another turn, while Aggie was arranging things. We looked into the church of St Vincent de Paul, where a Grand High Mass for the dead was being sung (it was All Souls Day). Afterwards we all went in an omnibus to the Champs Elysees. The bright sun gave the true Parisian gaiety to the streets as we drove along and it did the children good to run about in the gardens. The afternoon was spent quietly in the Hotel, and we left by the Lyons station at 8 p.m. for Turin, & the drive across Paris was a long one. During the afternoon the children were amused by what they saw from the hotel window, one cabman's blue hat with red cockade especially attracting them. They were also diverted by the crowds that continually were standing patiently awaiting their turn for the omnibuses. I was struck by the absence of priests and indeed all religious in the streets of Paris. I noticed an incident of French so-called politeness – a gentleman crossing the street takes off his hat to a lady and grasps her hand, but stands talking to her with his cigar in his mouth the whole time. "Le bon Diable" (the tailors' advertisement) seems to have departed this life and one of "Old England" is seen everywhere – a red cart, driven by a man in red coat with jockey's cap and with the horse half inside the cart, goes about stating that here "jerseys pour dames, demoiselles et fillettes" are to be had. Seeing Paris as it is now makes it most difficult to believe that only ten years ago the Germans marched in triumph through the streets. We found the porters at the Lyons Station most insolent and we had some difficulty about our tickets, but by speaking to the chef de gare we procured a reserved compartment so that we were able to settle ourselves comfortably for the night journey.

NOVEMBER 3, WEDNESDAY ♦ The children slept well and we all woke up near Macon, where the country was so covered with water that it looked like the deluge. There was lovely scenery afterwards of mountains and rich country covered with vineyards & near Culoz beautiful lakes. We found the provision basket that Edith had prepared for us most useful. As we approached the Alps we saw much snow which became more dense as we ascended. It was touching to see the children quietly settling for the night and saying their prayers as if in their nursery and adding "God bless us on our journey and bring us safely home", but they got very weary through the long day hours and we were quite glad to get out at Modane for the Douane and change of carriages. There was some bother about the two machines we had with us – a filter and a sewing machine – and we had duty to pay on each. We were revived by some soup before starting again and were once more fortunate in getting a carriage to ourselves. The passage through the Cenis tunnel is by no means unpleasant – not so bad indeed as the London underground railway. It was wet at Turin, but the next morning the roofs were covered in snow. The Grand Hotel de Turin is a very comfortable one – very large & well decorated. All the ceilings are painted by hand and some are very artistic. The agreeable landlord, a German, who was very kind to the children, showed me over most of the rooms. We all slept well after our long journey.

NOVEMBER 4 ♦ The next day was wet and cold, so the children did not get out, but Aggie and I took a walk through the principal streets. There is not much variety in them as Turin is almost entirely modern. We had left our luggage at the station, and so had only to have it registered direct for Rome at 7.30. Our start again promised well as we were put into a carriage direct for Rome all to ourselves. Again, all were settled for the night when in about an hour's time we were told that at Allessandria we must change carriages as the train was via Pisa and our tickets were via Bologna. So imagine the poor Babies being aroused and all the pillows, shawls & blankets hastily tied up and we emerge into semi-darkness at Allessandria with only a few minutes to get into another train. Imagine also a porter bearing our bundles which to our horror gradually come to pieces and drop, article by article, on to the crowded platform to be picked up as best we may, while we struggle with bags and babies. And worst of all, no empty carriage to be found, though we hear "partenza per Bologna" bells ringing. At last we are pitchforked into a carriage, bag & baggage, upon sleepy and protesting Italians three in number, a young man and woman and an old wretch who afterwards tried to avenge himself by attempting to persuade the guard that our tickets were insufficient in number. We arranged ourselves in the best way we could and were very thankful when our companions got out at Modena. The children thankfully managed to sleep in positions anything but conducive to repose. We were undisturbed in our carriage as far as Florence. We saw Pistoia and Prato, with its cathedral of white and black marble standing against the poetical sky. Poor Clement had caught cold in his eye and had to have it tied up for the journey. At last beautiful Florence and its graceful dome and towers come into view with Fiesole behind. We had time for a good breakfast of huge basins of coffee, rolls & butter, served by a man called Pietro, who I remembered at once as having been a waiter at the Caffè Greco in Rome. He knew me also and was astonished at the large family. As we breakfasted an aged flower "girl" almost covered us with flowers far beyond the value of the few pence I gave her, and insisted when we were in the train upon giving each of the children, even to dear baby, a bouquet. The little ones kissed their hands to bright Florence and we started for our last stage at 7.30 a.m. in a carriage to ourselves. The scenery was exquisite – the angry Arno flowing in a brown flood through hills studded with little towns of most picturesque outline and the blue mountains had clouds curling round their summits. It was now quite warm. At Arezzo I got some wine in one of those pretty bottles half covered with plaited work. At last is seen the Dome of St Peter's just visible over one of the flat ridges of the Campagna. A quiet sky of browny gold lay behind it, and soon the eternal city unfolds itself. Then we are at the grand old walls and soon within Rome. A passing glimpse of St John Lateran and we are at the station – here I notice a new Rome springing up all new to me. The hotel omnibus brought us quickly to the Hotel d'Italie and we are thankful to find ourselves arrived safely at our journey's end this fifth of November, which shall never be forgot ...

NOVEMBER 6, SATURDAY [AGNES WRITES] ♦ About 10.30 we all, under Mr Davies' escort, went to the Pincio with which we were delighted. Fountains splashed all around us under shady alcoves full of maiden hair & arum lilies, & nature seemed to welcome us on all sides with her brightest smiles. We left the children at play, & Mr Davies, Andrew, Mary and I went to the Piazza di Spagna to consult Mr Lowe at his Bureau as to apartments etc. Here I felt so tired that I could do no more, so Mary & I got into a fiacre & returned to the Hotel where I lay on my bed most of the day. Andrew was entertained at luncheon at the 'Greco' Trattoria by Mr Davies & in the afternoon they saw many rooms (none suitable however) & bought a perambulator for the children.

NOVEMBER 7, SUNDAY [ANDREW WRITES] ♦ After breakfast I went out to get some lotion and a shade for Clement's eyes. At eleven I took Bessie and Mary and Clement to the American church in the Via Nazionale – a really graceful building and good service, though the American prayer book is altered from our own in every way for the worse. The children like their table d'hôte dinner in the servants' salle. After luncheon Aggie and I drove to St Peter's and she was altogether charmed with the grandeur of the building and the associations connected with it. Then we drove to see very different buildings, and to think of other associations, in the Forum of Trajan, Foro Romano, Arch of Titus and Colosseum. We walked into the latter, which has changed its appearance much since I saw it in 1869. The excavations are very interesting, though I missed the stations and central cross. We drove back by the Fountain of Trevi and Aggie was fully delighted with what she had seen during the afternoon.

NOVEMBER 8, MONDAY   [ANDREW WRITES] ♦ Soon after breakfast I went to Davies' rooms in this street. He has a most characteristic room, fitted up with yellow of different tints and the ceiling coffered – when he had finished blacking his boots he and I started out in quest of apartments. We went first to some in the via Angelo Custode, which were full of old pictures and oggetti d'anticita [sic], but did not suit. Then we went to MacBean's bank where I presented my letter of introduction and got addresses of lodgings. We saw some most graceful and characteristic rooms at Via della Croce 44, with terraces and pretty views, kept by some pretty girls, but the rooms were too small. However, we got the address of some others in Via Babuino no. 151, which finally suited. Davies and I walked to the Pincio to find Aggie, but she had just left and on reaching the Hotel she told us of her morning's adventures – she and Bessie and the children had started off with the carrozzetta, nearly to the Pincio, when one of the wheels came off. Aggie in despair went to the first shop, which was an artist's colourman, and by signs made him understand what she wanted and at last got the wheel mended. At 12 o'clock Aggie and Davies & I walked towards Via Babuino where we happened to meet Miss Dawson, who told us of some rooms in the Via Sistino, so after Aggie had seen those in the via Babuino we went for luncheon to a trattoria in Via della Croce and afterwards to the Caffè Romano in the Corso, and Aggie much enjoyed her refreshments in such characteristic Roman places. Then we went to some shops and drove to Via Sistina. We found the rooms very nice, but far too dear, so drove back to Via Babuino where, after looking at some at no. 65 we returned to no.151, with which we were quite satisfied and agreed to take from tomorrow. We hope the sunny aspect and airy situation will prove a healthy home for our stay in Rome.

NOVEMBER 9, TUESDAY [ANDREW WRITES] ♦ After luncheon we all left the hotel in an omnibus and soon arranged our things in our new rooms at no. 151 Via Babuino 3° Piano. Davies called and helped me to order dinner for tomorrow at a trattoria, where afterwards Aggie and I dined, and had coffee at the Caffè Romano. Very warm night.

NOVEMBER 10, WEDNESDAY [AGNES WRITES] ♦ After breakfast we unpacked our filter & finding that something had gone wrong with the charcoal Andrew took it to the Chemists to have it seen to. During last night there was a fearful thunderstorm so the children did not go out this morning. The sun however soon became powerful & Andrew & I had to walk quite slowly. We went first to Mr Macbean & then in search of a basket for Baby to sleep in, as her cot has had to be devoted to Dollie. As we went to the Piazza Minerva we came to the Pantheon and Andrew & I went in and were overpowered by its marvellous grandeur. We heard a low Mass which was comforting. We looked with admiration at Raphael's tomb & each deposited a kiss on its alabaster tablet. We looked into many shops, bought our basket & got into a fiacre & returned to our house about 12.30. At 1 the man from the trattoria arrived with his tin case containing our excellent dinner! It was amusing to see the 'gusto' with which the chicks partook of the fare! First potage and pâtés d'Italie, then a side of Lamb & mashed potatoes, followed by an etherealised [sic] rice pudding & apples & pears! & some very good red ordinaire called "Vino di Castelli Romani". After luncheon we all went in a carriage to see Trajan's column, the Forum Romanum, the Colosseum, the Arches of Septimus Severus, Titus and Constantine, and thence to St Peter's. The children & Bessie were delighted with all they saw & they all duly kissed the foot of St Peter's statue & were intensely interested & very intelligent. Mr Davies came in afterwards & sat an hour & saw all the chicks before they went to bed. We had a nice supper of macaroni, frita of brains & some veal. Paid for our first month's lodgings & interviewed our very pleasant padrone, Signor Callus, who also brought some beautiful water colour designs for mosaics done by his son for us to see.

NOVEMBER 11 [ANDREW WRITES] ♦ Dora was not quite well so Aggie stayed with her. I walked with the other children as far as the Pincio then left them with Bessie and called at the Hotel D'Italie and afterwards looked for some subjects to paint. Davies called to ask me to go with him in the afternoon. So I accordingly joined him at the Caffè degli Artisti and with some others we walked to the Trastevere where we saw a large collection of rather doubtful antique statues belonging to Torlonia. I came back in a cab. Aggie took the three elder children out.

NOVEMBER 12, FRIDAY [AGNES WRITES] ♦ We were amused to see an inscription over a Dairy namely (sic) "English Dairy. Freshmil Kcream – Eggs"!! We suppose the words were written down for them & they not in the least understanding them have thus divided the word!

NOVEMBER 14, SUNDAY [ANDREW WRITES] ♦ Aggie and I took a little walk later on and went into the church of San Lorenzo in Lucina. We twice saw horses fall

THE PANTHEON IN ROME. THE DONALDSONS WERE VERY MOVED BY RAPHAEL'S TOMB

down in the street today and noticed the cruelty with which they were used. No attempt being made to help them out of the harness. Roman nurses in their gay ribbons and gold pins attracted Aggie's attention. Leonard was much struck by the gens d'armes' "cock-hats" as he called them.

As they settled into life in Rome, Andrew continued to paint and sketch, and they decided to learn Italian.

NOVEMBER 16 [ANDREW WRITES] ♦ As my cold was no better I stayed in all day. Aggie went out with the children in the morning. Miss Dawson and two Italian governesses sent by her called – the latter wretched specimens of the race, one old and sour, the other young but vulgar.

NOVEMBER 18, THURSDAY [ANDREW WRITES] ♦ We had another bad night from my cough. I stayed in doors all day. An Italian lady (Mde Lana) came in morning and we engaged her to give us Italian lessons twice a week.

NOVEMBER 19, FRIDAY [ANDREW WRITES] ♦ My cough as bad as ever at night. Signora called (our Padrona) to enquire after my cold and was very pleased with Baby. Aggie had her first lesson in Italian in the evening and we liked the mistress.

NOVEMBER 20, SATURDAY [AGNES WRITES] ♦ Andrew a little better, but still coughing a good deal & Clement & Leonard & Dollie all coughing a little. So they none of them went out. After breakfast Mary & I went to the Via dei Condotti to get some medicine for Andrew, and then on past the Piazza della Colonna to buy some Roman dolls for her and Dollie which I had noticed there before as being cheap. I saw a young girl who was sent here from the Hotel d'Italie, a certain Elvira Spadi, who came with a good recommendation from an English lady with whom she had lived a year, & who wished a situation as under nurse. We have engaged her for 3 ½ months.

NOVEMBER 21, SUNDAY, EVE OF ST CECILIA [AGNES WRITES] ♦ After luncheon I took Mary & Clement with me to St Cecilia's basilica. We arrived early & so looked about the church well before Benediction began. I shall never forget the impression of seeing the marble figure of the saint lying beneath the high altar. It is the figure of a very small, slight woman with the most delicate feet and hands & the poor little head piteously turned away showing the gashed throat. It brought tears to one's eyes. The church was crowded with priests, monks, nuns, confraternities, students in red, students in purple, students in black and red, students in black and blue etc. Contadini, poor people of the city &

kindred persons of every shade of society & a few forestieri. The Baldachino was simply one mass of tapers, piled up tier upon tier to the ceiling, & 2 huge candelabra bearing each one immense candles stood in a line with the altar. Benediction began with a procession round the church with the B. Sacrament & the 'Salutaris Hostia' was exquisitely sung by the Papal Choir. Before the Litany began the Tenor in a loud ringing voice to a simple Gregorian ordering of notes cried aloud "Sancta Cecilia ora pro nobis" & the whole vast congregation fell on their knees! It was a thrilling moment.

going to Mass

NOVEMBER 24, WEDNESDAY [AGNES WRITES] ♦ Leonard was poorly with a cold so he stayed at home with me. The others were out all morning till 12, when I took the lessons. A lady (name unknown!) called to ask me if I would undertake to educate her little boy with ours! Which offer I declined with thanks!

NOVEMBER 25, THURSDAY [ANDREW WRITES] ♦ I went to the Pincio to finish the subject I began last week. Aggie took Baby to be photographed with her in the Via Condotti. In the afternoon Aggie & I drove on the Via Appia. It was a lovely soft afternoon and the tombs and beautiful mountains showed their very best effects. We saw the chapel of the "Domine, Quo Vadis", Arch of Drusus, tomb of Cecilia Metella, Basilica of San Sebastiano and the churches of San Giorgio in Velabro & San Gregoriano. On our way back, we did some shopping and Clement was struck by the resemblance of an oriental bishop we met in the Piazza di Spagna to 'Father Christmas'.

NOVEMBER 30, ST ANDREW'S DAY [ANDREW WRITES] ♦ Aggie and I drove to the church of St Andrea della Valle, where we heard a mass, and afterwards we looked at shops in the neighbourhood and got some presents. In passing through the market near the Pantheon we saw a porcupine hanging up at a butchers with all quills on, deer, cranes and other strange creatures.

DECEMBER 4 [ANDREW WRITES] ♦ The children went out twice and in the afternoon were much pleased by riding in a goat tram-way on the Pincio. Dolly announced dinner to me this morning "Panzo e ponto" (pranzo e pronto).

DECEMBER 8, WEDNESDAY, FEAST OF THE IMMACULATE CONCEPTION [ANDREW WRITES] ♦ Shops were nearly all shut, but Aggie after waiting some time managed to get Mary's and Dora's photographs done at Suscipj's. In the afternoon we drove to the Forum and saw the interesting church of Sta Francesca Romana and afterwards went to Ara Coeli where there was a grand function – a great crowd of people, many lights and processions. There was a glorious sunset as we descended the slightly dangerous steps of Ara-coeli. The children went to the Pincio in the afternoon and found it crowded – Rome altogether has been en fête. Bells beginning to ring at 4 o'clock a.m. and going on more or less all day.

DECEMBER 19 [ANDREW WRITES] ♦ Aggie and I went to early communion. The elder children went to church with me at 11. In the afternoon Aggie and I and Clement went to St Peter's and heard Vespers and Compline – we walked about the church both before and after the service examining the chapels and monuments. A showery day. Dora went out with Elvira. In the evening a messenger brought an invitation for an Audience with the Pope tomorrow.

Andrew and Agnes belonged to the Church of England, but favoured its 'High Church' side. They were impressed by the Catholic ceremonies they saw in Rome, and their private audience with Pope Leo XIII was clearly a highlight of their stay.

DECEMBER 20 [AGNES WRITES] ♦ At 11 o'clock Andrew and I left in a nice carriage for the Vatican. I wore my black velvet dress & black lace veil & he was in full evening dress. When we arrived at the entrance the Swiss guard presented arms and then we alighted and went up flight after flight of hard white marble steps until at last we arrived in a large vestibule where many servants in gorgeous medieval dresses of crimson flowered satin met us, and when they saw our letter of introduction was correct showed us into a huge hall, where we were received & led to seats by a most pleasant and sweet looking young ecclesiastic of about 22 or 23 in violet. Here we sat for an hour & quarter. The hall was decorated with huge pictures of sacred subjects. A throne under a Baldachino was at the end and an immense & magnificent ivory crucifix was at the other. Grand majordomos walked about & spoke to persons of high rank. A monsignor sat next to me & talked a little to me very pleasantly in Italian. At last a move was made – a door opened & after a few mysterious signs about 12 people went from the hall where we were sitting through a red door into another room, & in time each batch of people had their turn. Most people took something to be blessed, but some took huge boxes of rosaries & others had bunches of some 6 or a dozen rosaries in their hands until all the medals and crosses on them rang like bells! At last our turn came! We passed through the red door & found ourselves in a large hall where more of the gorgeous crimson servants stood who showed us into a "stanzi" along which we walked in pairs.

Then there was a crimson curtain – & through that we passed & were actually in the presence of the "Santo Padre". He was seated by the side of a small table on which was a large crucifix & his gorgeous crimson hat trimmed with gold. He was in white silk from head to – well, not to foot because that was a crimson velvet slipper with a gold cross on it, & it was on a cushion a little raised so as easily to be kissed. On his right side stood a Cardinal in violet robes (it being Advent) who announced the names & the country of each set of people who came up. A large crimson cushion was in front of the Pope & as soon as our names were announced Andrew & I knelt down & the Pope immediately gave us his right hand to kiss (to kiss the large episcopal ring – it was an immense amethyst). Then he took Andrew's hand in his right hand & mine in his left & held them all the time he was talking to us. He spoke in Italian. He first asked if Andrew had been in Rome before & then he asked how long we were going to stay – & gave his blessing on the visit – then I said we were here with our five little children & he blessed them. Then Andrew said he was a painter & he said with a bright winning smile "Oh then Rome is the right place for you. There are so many beautiful things to paint here". He then laid his hands on our heads and blessed us & we kissed his hand & his foot & the audience was over! We passed out by a door at the side which opened onto the broad marble staircase & on descending we quickly found our carriage & drove home. Never can we forget this great event ...

DECEMBER 22, WEDNESDAY [ANDREW WRITES] ♦ Fine day with cold wind. I had a good morning at my street subject – Aggie paid the books. The children got out. In the afternoon, Clement and Leonard went with us to a shop in the Ripetta to buy sweetmeats and a cake for Xmas, we returned by the Corso.

DECEMBER 25, SATURDAY, CHRISTMAS DAY [AGNES WRITES] ♦ Andrew and I went to the Early Communion at 8.30. Before we went I went to the children who were enjoying the treasures which they had found in their stockings! We took Mary, Clement & Leonard to Church at 11 & after dinner we took them to Araceoli where they were enchanted at hearing little children recite the Story of Bethlehem on a platform & they also saw the 'Presepio' which really was very pretty. At tea the children had an iced cake & then they came into the drawing room & had crackers & games till 7. Mr Davies & Mr Barclay came to dinner & Mr Davies gave us all nice presents. After dinner we sat round a nice cheerful wood fire & talked & had some music & all agreed that we had had a very happy day.

DECEMBER 29 [ANDREW WRITES] ♦ As the morning was damp I was busy cutting drawings off boards and laying down fresh paper. I went out to pay the weekly books. In the afternoon the two boys went out with me. We crossed the Tiber by the ugly new bridge from the Ripetta and found a good view of St Peter's and the Castle of St Angelo on the other side. I deplored the new buildings arising on the Prati so that in a short time the views of St Peter's from the river bank will be no more. As we returned Clement chose a silk handkerchief as his present for Mr Smart. We bought also a knitted jacket for Baby. We also looked into a church (S. Madelena). The other children went out with Bessie and Elvira.

DECEMBER 31, FRIDAY [ANDREW WRITES] ♦ We finish up this year happily in Rome our expedition thus far having been successful and we trust we shall accomplish the rest of our Italian life during the early months of the New Year with equal success. Italian lesson in the evening.

JANUARY 1 1881 [AGNES WRITES] ♦ Andrew gave me a lovely bouquet of snowdrops & one white camellia in the centre before I was up this morning, & after breakfast Bessie gave me a sweet bunch of pink roses & some very sweet smelling kind of small white narcissus. The children all went out in the morning, & again in the afternoon, with the exception of dear Phoebe who stayed with me.

JANUARY 3, MONDAY [ANDREW WRITES] ♦ I went out before luncheon to the Post Office and in the afternoon explored the old streets in search of subjects. I studied the old Pescheria near the Ghetto. It is most picturesque with its dark arches and overhanging balconies and crumbling marble slabs and the columns of the Portico of Octavia in front all combine to make a curious mixture of ruined grandeur, dirt and picturesque squalor. I passed through the Piazza Navona where is now the annual fair held at this time. Much like other fairs with shows of Giants, fat-women, double-babies &c. Shops are erected all over the Piazza and all sorts of cheap articles are to be had. Our Italian lesson in the evening.

JANUARY 6, THE EPIPHANY [AGNES WRITES] ♦ Such a night as we had! Pouring rain, and deafening noises of penny whistles, trumpets, drums, crowing like cocks until 4 a.m. & then beginning again at 6 a.m. This is the Roman people's way of celebrating the Epiphany or the 'Befano' as they call it. Certainly it is not a custom to be imitated! At 10 Andrew and I went to the Greek Church to a Grand High Mass. A most curious ceremony it was, and the ritual and ceremonial generally so complicated as to make the grandest Roman function appear simple, & yet it lacked the grandeur & dignity of the Roman Rite. Still, I am glad to have seen it, as it is most curious. Out of Aunt Jane's Christmas present we treated ourselves to a drive in the afternoon.

JANUARY 10 [AGNES WRITES] ♦ Andrew and I took the 4 elder children out for a walk in the morning. They were delighted at seeing in the Via Dei Condotti in a florist's window a peacock (life size) made entirely out of flowers. The neck and breast were shaded violets, the wings green & the full outspread tail was wonderfully imitated with pansies & variegated geranium leaves.

JANUARY 17, MONDAY, ST ANTHONY'S DAY [AGNES WRITES] ♦ Andrew and I went to see the animals blessed at S. Vito's & a curious ceremony it was. We saw a little dog blessed in the church & then the priest came outside & blessed the cab horses which were outside.

FEBRUARY 3

[ANDREW WRITES] In the evening we went to a ball at the German embassy. The guests were entirely Germans and the male portion were largely decorated with stars and crosses and  ribbons. We remarked some extraordinarily large people of both sexes. It was a gay and brilliant scene and we were amused. The rooms of the Palazzo Caffarelli are very handsome especially the large hall in which the ambassador and his wife received the guests.

FEBRUARY 7 [ANDREW WRITES] ♦ My birthday. In the evening we went to the Argentina Theatre and heard the opera 'Il Barbiere di Seviglia' very well performed. This was followed by a spectacle of the campaign of Napoleon in Russia. The military dresses were very good. We had some chocolate at a caffè afterwards. We felt quite dissipated walking in the streets of Rome at midnight. The Pantheon looked very grand in the moonlight as we passed it.

FEBRUARY 23 [ANDREW WRITES] ♦ A very lovely day. I finished my drawing at the Marmorata. I very much enjoyed my morning. The sun was strong shining out of a clear blue sky. I noticed an almond tree on the Aventine full in blossom,

standing out against the blue like a tree in frosted silver. Several Observanti frati passed and were highly complimentary in their remarks about my drawing.

Carnivals took place before Lent began.

FEBRUARY 23, WEDNESDAY [AGNES WRITES] ♦ Mary's cold kept her in doors all day, poor little girl. She was so wonderfully good about not going to the Carnival & never made the slightest fuss. I stayed with her in the morning while Bessie went out with the others & then when she came in I went out with Clement to the Piazza Navona to buy a night lamp. [Andrew continues later] Mary was not well enough to go to the Carnival show, but was a very good girl and Aggie rewarded her with a doll. All the rest of us went to our balcony. Today (Giovedi Grasso) was the great day of the carnival and it was really worth seeing. There was a splendid procession of mounted men in real moorish dress with harness and trapping all real and good. Also one in chain armour. Moorish ladies carried in palanquins and camels – another good show was that of the French Academy with a gorgeous car filled with students in white dresses of the time of Henri III. This was preceded by riders. Then there was a comic procession of cooks very funny and an admirable carriage drawn by men with horses' heads. The Corso was full and the masks were numerous and quaint – we were all much amused.

MARCH 5, SATURDAY [AGNES WRITES] ♦ I went to do a little shopping, then came in and did some packing. After dinner took charge of Baby while Bessie took Mary & Dollie out for a turn. Elvira took the boys to the Pincio twice today.

MARCH 6, SUNDAY [AGNES WRITES] ♦ Our last Sunday in Rome! Well it was a lovely spring day & we made the most of it. Andrew & I went to the Early Communion & I stayed with Baby and Dollie & Andrew took Mary, Clement and Leonard to church at 11 o'clock. After dinner he and I took them first to drink of Trevi & then to Vespers at St Peter's. The music was beautiful (I think it was Palestrina's) but I felt so choking with the feeling of its being the last time – that it was almost a painful pleasure. We visited affectionately every corner of the building & at last tore ourselves reluctantly away.

MARCH 7, MONDAY [ANDREW WRITES] ♦ Our last day in Rome! And a lovely sunny one it has been. We were very busy packing all the morning. Just before going to bed Clement solemnly presented his beloved hobby-horse to the little boy on the piano above us. We all felt very sad at leaving dear Rome, where we have had four months of uninterrupted happiness.

MARCH 8, TUESDAY [ANDREW WRITES] ♦ We had a compartment in the train to ourselves. As we flew through the Campagna we gazed fondly at St Peter's and gave a longing last look at the cupola as it finally disappeared. At Orvieto we purchased a fiasco of refreshing wine. The children enjoyed their dinner on the train. After some afternoon hours of strong sun we began to look out for Florence and were very glad to arrive – we had some waiting at the station to get our luggage and were all tired and glad to get to bed soon after supper. The Hotel Montebello seems likely to suit, being exquisitely clean and bright and cheerful.

The family stayed in Florence for six weeks. As well as sightseeing and exploring the spring countryside, Andrew painted scenes in the city, including the Ponte Vecchio.

MARCH 23, WEDNESDAY [AGNES WRITES] ♦ Our dear Mary's birthday. She had many nice presents and was very happy. After luncheon we had the most delightful drive to Fiesole. The boys were delighted at our coachman allowing them to sit on the box & drive in turns (viz hold the reins) as the horse crept slowly up the zig zag road! When we reached Fiesole the male part of our party visited the Reformed Franciscan monastery, whilst we sat on a bench and gazed at the beautiful view, & also bought some little baskets ... We then went to a restaurant & had some lemonade & sponge cakes and got back by ¼ to 6 after a perfect afternoon.

APRIL 19, TUESDAY [ANDREW WRITES] ♦ We were up before five and got all ready – a wet day! Which we were rather glad to see. We got a through compartment to Venice. We gazed at the Duomo for the last time – Florence looked melancholy in the rain and grey mist. We eagerly look out for Venice and at last see the campanile and are soon rushing through the lagoon. The children were delighted with the gondola that took us from the station to the Hotel and in our way we saw part of the Grand Canal – Rialto, Bridge of Sighs etc. In the evening Aggie and I strolled into the piazza and she got an idea of Venice before going to bed. To which haven we were all glad to retire very early.

The Donaldsons spent a month in Venice. Although they enjoyed the beautiful city, with gondola rides and all the historic sights, which Andrew painted, they were not fond of their hotel, and unluckily fell quite ill.

APRIL 28, THURSDAY [ANDREW WRITES] ♦ We are fortunate in having the dreariness of our Table d'Hôte relieved by seeing the gorgeous effect every night on S. Giorgio. Its blood red campanile with white stone and dark copper spire stand out in rich tone against the deep blue sky. The children saw the picturesque funeral of one of the canons of S. Marco, with cross, acolytes & priests in one gondola; and the vestments of the deceased over the covering of the coffin in another. They also saw a man arrested by gens d'armes who crept behind him & seized him by his ears.

MAY 7, SATURDAY [ANDREW WRITES] ♦ Aggie was very unwell in the night about 12 and greatly alarmed me with difficulty of breathing from her sore throat. Bessie made her a hot poultice and I went out for some ice, which remedies somewhat relieved her. Still she has been very poorly and weak all day. She got up in the afternoon. I went to finish my subject of Venice from the quay. In the afternoon I took the whole party with Bessie in the gondola – we went first near La Madonna del Orto and then by the Misericordia into the Lagoon – the water for the first time was as clear as glass and we thoroughly enjoyed gliding along in the warm sunlight but very much missed "Mam-a". Before going to bed Aggie enjoyed seeing the gondolas gliding about, each with its little light. Venice certainly is a dream-city, which might vanish at any moment.

MAY 8, SUNDAY [ANDREW WRITES] ♦ Aggie's throat was again so painful in the night that I went out before 9 o'clock to fetch Dottore Richetti, who came and relieved our minds about there being anything of a diphtheric

ANDREW DESCRIBED VENICE AS A 'DREAM-CITY, WHICH MIGHT VANISH AT ANY MOMENT'

nature in the attack, and he suggested the same treatment which Aggie had been using. Most inconveniently I also began with one of the worst headaches I have ever had. I struggled to go out in a gondola with the three elder children for a short time – the exercise is certainly the most bearable under the circumstance, but for the rest of the day I was prostrate.

MAY 12, THURSDAY [ANDREW WRITES] ♦ Aggie and I much better. We went to the Bank and then to the Railway Station to try and get through tickets which we were not able to obtain. Then to the market near the Rialto where I purchased some milk and eggs for the journey.

MAY 13, FRIDAY [ANDREW WRITES] ♦ After luncheon I induced Aggie to come in the gondola and she was much refreshed after her long confinement in her room. My throat became sore and ulcerated and we were trying remedies the rest of the afternoon. The children had a treat in being taken over Sir W. Scott's steam yacht by his chief engineer, who had taken a fancy to them and also to Bessie, and showed this later on by bringing Bessie a handsome locket and chain. Sailor generosity! as he probably would never see her again.

MAY 14, SATURDAY [ANDREW WRITES] ♦ My throat very bad. We got up early. I went on a barca with the luggage and the rest followed in Gasparo's gondola. We found we could only take tickets to Turin. As we approached Turin we enjoyed seeing the snowy Alps which looked very grand against a quiet yellow sky. As soon as we arrived Aggie commenced vigorous measures for my throat and I got rapidly better. We felt quite like going home to the comfortable Grand Hotel de Turin, where the landlord and his servants welcomed us as old friends and were very attentive.

Their journey home was complicated by a landslip in the Alps, which affected the railway line and forced passengers to go part of the way by road.

MAY 16, MONDAY [ANDREW WRITES] ♦ All up at three a.m. At the station we had a great fuss. First because Aggie had to wait for her bag at the hotel and we nearly missed each other, then because they would not allow us to bring any small baggage into the train. At last after almost giving up the baggage in despair I got it through by bribery and corruption. At Chiamonte everything was disorganised and I had to pick out our luggage as best I could. When this was done it was all tied behind the queer "landau" with four horses which was awaiting us. It was amusing to see all the mule wagons, carriages and omnibuses and even donkey carts with sofas and chairs in them which were all assembled to take the passengers. Our four horses soon took the lead and we got to San Bertrand on good time to register our luggage and take our tickets to Modane and also to get a very good breakfast at the little inn. Clement and Leonard much enjoyed the drive, sitting with me in the banquette – the drive was most refreshing. There was a frightful confusion at Modane. The number of Paris carriages was not sufficient. There was little time to do all that had to be done, to collect the luggage that was hopelessly scattered about and have it examined by the Douanes and afterwards to get it registered to Paris and to get fresh tickets. However, we got off all right ...

Exhausted by the journey they reached Paris in the early morning, and after some breakfast at their hotel they went to bed for an hour or two.

MAY 17, TUESDAY [ANDREW WRITES] ♦ Aggie and I strolled out and looked at the shops – she bought herself a pretty shaded red hat, and socks and shoes for Phoebe's birthday. In the afternoon we had a carriage and the whole party drove to Notre Dame.

Next day they caught the train to the Channel ferry.

MAY 18, WEDNESDAY [AGNES WRITES] ♦ Bessie and I were very ill indeed. However, Folkestone was reached at last and after a cup of tea we started. I was very ill again in the train. At Charing Cross the dearest Father and Artie met us and we got into an omnibus & we and the Father went off at once to Newburgh House whilst Andrew sent the luggage & then he and Artie followed us in a hansom. Thank God we are safely home after 7 most happy & blessed months – blessed with happiness and with health almost uninterruptedly – DEO GRATIAS.

Evidently the Donaldsons thoroughly enjoyed their travels, robustly surmounting the difficulties of railway journeys with so much luggage and five children under the age of eight, not to mention the inevitable ailments that one or another of the party suffered from while they were away. Back in London, the Donaldsons continued to write their joint diary entries until Agnes's death in August 1918. Andrew continued the diary alone until he fell ill and died in April 1919. Their daughter Phoebe contributed the last entries describing his final days, when 'All his wanderings were of pictures and painting.'

ST THOMAS'S HOSPITAL
Peter King and nurses

The famous London teaching hospital, St Thomas's, was at the forefront of medical treatment in the late Victorian period. We can get some flavour of its everyday life from the following diaries, the first from a patient, the rest from nurses at work there.

Peter King was a patient at St Thomas's in the spring of 1885; he had been treated there previously for a leg ulcer which was still causing him trouble. His clear description of life in the ward from a patient's viewpoint dovetails well with the nurses' accounts of the same routines just over a decade later. His graphic account of his operation is not for the squeamish, who will be particularly horrified by the surgeon's decision, apparently on a whim, not to bother with anaesthetic after all.

Florence Nightingale, the great nursing reformer, set up her nurses' training school at St Thomas's in 1860. It soon gained a high reputation for producing excellent nurses who were in demand throughout the medical world for their skill and professionalism. Thirty-seven years into the history of the establishment, Florence Nightingale – now aged 77 and in poor health – still took an active interest in 'her' nurses. The head of the school reported regularly to her, and in 1897 she sent her a batch of probationers' ward diaries. These ward diaries were regarded as part of the new recruits' training; a month to six weeks after they had enrolled, they were asked to write down the events of a day on their ward. The workload was heavy and the hours long, but the nurses' pride in their work comes across loud and clear, as do their sympathy for the patients and their emphasis on rigorous cleanliness. 'Stone-cloths' were nappies.

AN OPERATION AT CHARING CROSS HOSPITAL

PETER KING

Peter King was not overjoyed to be back at St Thomas's in the spring of 1885.

MARCH 31 1885 ◆ Once more after an absence of 18 months, I am compelled to seek the skill of the splendid Institution of St Thomas' Hospital. How long I may be detained within its walls, God alone knows. I am again placed in Leopold ward, and by a singular coincidence, the same bed, so that Number 13 sounds familiar.

APRIL 1 ◆ The first night is over, and I am getting more used to my changed circumstances. I spent a rather restless night, looking round at the sleepers, and living my last visit over again ... At 5 o'clock, breakfast is brought round, and at 6 o'clock we wash. 7 o'clock brings the day nurses into the ward, and the work of bedmaking and tidying the ward commences. At 8 o'clock Sister enters the ward and reads morning prayers, after which 'dressing' begins, and medicine is received from Sister. A second breakfast of bread and milk is served at 9.30. Today the ward has been scrubbed, and the floors, being of solid oak, polished. At 1 o'clock the bell rings for dinner, and the ward remains quiet till three. This is Visitors' Day, and I receive a visit from my sister. The time went all too quickly, and when 4.30 chimed out from Big Ben, the visitors left. Tea followed, and at 5.30 we had prayers presided over by Sister who also accompanied the singing of some half dozen hymns on the harmonium, a fitting close to the day, for at this time the shadows are lengthening, and the sun sinking in the west. The appropriate prayers and hymns and the quietude all seem in keeping with the hospital, and we can hardly realise that we are in the heart of the Metropolis. From six till eight the nurses are busy 'dressing', after which the ward is put in order, and as the clock strikes eight the gas is lowered, and we bid each other goodnight.

APRIL 2, THURSDAY ◆ After a restless night I awoke about four. I with several others was visited by a nurse and given some physic. I thought that this betokened an operation, but it was not so. In the afternoon, I saw for the first time the eminent surgeon Sir William McCormack, who is a fine man standing over six feet. He is a most distinguished man, having been at Sedan and Metz. He has served in many parts of the world, and is the author of many celebrated works which have been published in French, German, Dutch and Russian. There were two operations performed in the bathroom, Number 18 and my neighbour Number 14. The smell of ether was very strong and unpleasant, it being familiar to me after three operations. Sir William walked round the ward and after examining me, he said "This abscess must be opened" (the abscess was in my leg). I feared that I should have to wait several days, but at tea time Sister told me that I was to have no supper as they were going to perform the operation under chloroform. She said that I might expect the House Surgeon about nine. When the lights were lowered, and silence reigned, I awaited his arrival. Nine struck, and then a quarter past, and then half past. I heard footsteps approaching, and was soon surrounded by Sister, Staff Nurse, Surgeon and assistants. I asked if I was to have chloroform, and he said "No, I will do it without". I lay on my side and the sensation was not pleasant while he was finding the place to cut, and getting the knife ready. At length I felt the cold steel. It was not just lancing, but deliberate cutting, and that deep too. Then a drainage tube was put in. All this was done under a carbolic spray. The dressing consisted of a wool bag, gauze bandages and wadding, and yards of flannel. After this performance, I felt somewhat exhausted, and Sister gave me some brandy and water, after which I lay down, and with difficulty got to sleep.

APRIL 3 ♦ Today is Good Friday, and treated in Hospital exactly as a Sunday. The dressers do not come, and Sister does not enter the ward till later. Shortly before eleven we had service. Sister presided. We commenced by singing the Passion hymn 'O come and mourn with me awhile'. We had Morning Prayer and the proper Psalms and lessons followed by the hymn 'When I survey the wondrous Cross'. We should have had some more hymns had not the surgeon come up to perform an operation on a little boy who had been run over on Clapham Common by a bolting horse. Three other little boys were also hurt. One died shortly after admission. One was discharged, and the other is in a dangerous condition. They were only six years old.

APRIL 4, SATURDAY ♦ Nothing particular happened today beyond an operation in the afternoon. Number 9, a young fisherman from the North Sea fisheries, who had an injury to his arm. The trolley came up for him and took him to the theatre. When he was coming round he sang one of Sankey's hymns, 'Verily verily ye must be born again', the words being very distinct.

APRIL 5, EASTER DAY ♦ The day opens fine. At our morning service we sang Easter hymns, such as 'Jesus Christ is risen today'. The ward was beautifully decorated with spring flowers and potted plants which gave a nice cheerful appearance and reminded us of the country.

APRIL 6, EASTER MONDAY ♦ Nurse O'Brien tells me there are a great number of people on the water, as well as in the streets. She has been to South Kensington during her three hours off. This nurse recently came from Ireland, as her name implies as well as her accent. She is a very vivacious, happy and agreeable

PETER KING AND HIS WIFE NURSE O'BRIEN
AFTER HIS STAY AT ST THOMAS'S

LEOPOLD WARD IN ST THOMAS'S HOSPITAL, WHERE PETER KING STAYED

young lady. I was dressed again antiseptically, and the tube in my wound changed for a smaller one. I read a great deal of Bleak House as I am recovering from my indisposition of the last few days. The gaslight is hardly strong enough, so about seven I gave up. At about 7.30 the nurses go round the ward arranging each bed for the night, unpinning the quilts and turning them down.

APRIL 7, TUESDAY ♦ 'Accident week' has commenced. The various wards take it in turn to receive accidents, so that all accidents this week will be received in Leopold Ward. During the day several are admitted. They are attended to immediately and then washed. Broken legs are put in plaster in the bathroom. I woke up in the night, and seeing lights in the bathroom and hearing voices, I concluded there had been an accident. On looking at Big Ben, I saw that it was a quarter past two. A young man was wheeled into the ward. He had been stabbed in the side and hand during a quarrel.

My neighbour Number 14 is getting worse. About ten the next morning Mr Makins the Surgeon ordered his removal to another ward, Erysipelas having set in. The Sister had the place sprinkled with carbolic acid, and ordered that my dressing was not to be changed that day. His place was taken by a little boy named Albert Edward. He was six years old and his leg had been broken by a kick from another boy. In the afternoon the visitors came, mine being a sister and a friend from the office.

Next day was Sir William's day, and soon after ten he walks accompanied by a group of students. He takes his time and delivers quite a lecture on the various cases. He examined me, used a probe, and said there must be a diseased bone in my leg which had better be opened. I told him of my previous operations, and that I had not really come in for that. He said "You must please yourself". This set me thinking as to whether it was worthwhile undergoing another operation as the others had been unsuccessful. Were there much chance of success, I would not hesitate. I may be laid up for months and perhaps lose my situation. I think I will decline it.

Peter King was perhaps justified in his decision to decline a further operation, for he lived to a fine old age, dying at 82 in 1941. He married vivacious Nurse O'Brien two years after his spell in St Thomas's, and they had a happy life together until she died, also at 82, in 1940. Their daughter, Miss Frances King, made the diary available to the St Thomas's Hospital house journal, Circle, *in 1972, but its current whereabouts are unknown.*

VIOLET M. WILSON

Entered Hospital March 31 1896

OCTOBER 8 1896, CHILDREN'S WARD VICTORIA ♦ I went on duty at 7 a.m. Washed, dressed and took the temperatures of five children. Then I helped night-nurse to dress a mastoid case and when she dispensed with my help I went and put a fresh antiseptic dressing on what had been an abscess on the buttock of a convalescent typhoid case. After I had cleared away all the soiled dressings & mopped out the stone-cloths I started to dust the middle of the ward & washing Sister's and the wine table, the centre table and cabinet, polishing the top of the fireplaces and pipes. When I had finished dusting I filled the Lotion Bottles for the Spray Table and washed the wine glasses. As I had the short morning off duty it was my work to boil the syringes, fill the Boiler and Sterilizer, give out the toys to the children and finally sweep up the crumbs the children had made during lunch all of which I did and came off duty at 10 a.m.

I returned to the ward at 12.30 and helped Nurse to prepare the children's dinner, took round the milks, and mince for those on full diet and fed those who were unable to feed themselves. When dinner was over I made the nine children I was responsible for tidy and comfortable and then dusted down the side of the ward. At 2.30 the food for the children under 1 year was brought in and I fed two babies. After the feedings were finished I cleared all the things away, washed the feeding bottles and left them to soak in water. Having a little spare time, I looked over some sheets, put those that required darning to one side and put the rest to air, then sat and sewed until a quarter to 4 p.m. when I helped to give the children's teas round. As I had a short time to spare before 5 p.m. I commenced to put my children to bed (i.e. changed their day clothes, put the night blanket next to them & took off the white quilts, filled the various hot water bottles) and took their temperatures. At 5 p.m. I went off duty for tea and returned to the ward at 5.30 p.m. when I prepared the Feedings and helped to feed the Babies, washed the feeding bottles & cleared away the mugs, spoons etc. Then I put the rest of my children to bed, put away the toys & made the middle of the ward tidy. I then helped Staff Nurse to water the plants and by the time we had finished it was 7.30 p.m. At that time the last Feedings for the day were due and after I had helped to feed the Babies and made them comfortable it was 8.15 p.m. Shortly afterwards Sister came into the ward and after I had given my report I came off duty.

L. M. Shebbeare — Diary — Entered Mar: 25:96.
Med: Male George ———— December 2. 1896.

We all started for our Wards as the
Clock struck 7. — Being on day
nurses side I helped her to make
beds for the first 3/4 of an hour
I then tidyed up the soild bed
clothes we had left behind us &
washed one patient before prayers
at 8. o'clk. for which we all collect
at the centre pipes —
After prayers I carried up the poringers
& other things to the lavitory washed
them & brought them back, put
a dressing on one patients feet &
legs, rubbed all the backs with
spirit & powder & after putting all
the beds & lockers straight & making
all the side tidy began the
dusting — which is done in George
first with hot water & then polished
up with a dry duster —

PAGE FROM A NURSE'S WARD DIARY

MISS E. KNIGHT
Entered Hospital June 26 1896

OCTOBER 24 1896, CHILDREN'S WARD VICTORIA ♦ Commenced at 7 a.m. by washing 15 and 16, two little girls, one suffering from hip disease who has an extension, the other from abscess on back, washed and combed their heads with dust-comb, dressed them, made their beds & took temperatures. Then went over to other side of the ward & washed 5, a boy with hip disease whose leg has an extension on. Went to table for prayers. Washed & dressed 6, a boy who is now convalescent after operation on cleft palate & is allowed to get up & run about, and 9, a boy with tubercular elbow, which is supported in a sling, washed & combed heads, took temperatures & made their beds. Filled a hotwater bottle for one of the babies, finishing by 8.30.

Dusted down both sides of the ward & small ward. Cleaned the bathroom, polishing taps, washing & drying basins, oiling slabs & wiping down window ledges, & tidied up generally. Scrubbed 3 sheet mackintoshes & 6 or 7 small ones. Changed the stone-cloths & gave bedpans to the children all down night nurse's side of ward, finishing by 10.15.

Looked through some clean bibs, putting aside those that needed mending, and went off duty at 10.30. Back in ward at 1.30. Made my six little patients clean for the afternoon, washing faces & hands, brushing hair, changing stone-cloths & putting clean pinafores on those who needed them. Filled jugs on spray & doctor's tables, washed wine-glasses & made up the fire. Carbolized & put away dressing mackintoshes & put away clean stonecloths.

Helped to tidy cupboards & sat down at table to pad splints until 3.45. Tied bibs on the children, gave plates for tea, fed two children with bread & milk and helped to feed the other helpless patients. Put two of my children to bed, lit the gases in ward, lavatory & bathroom and went to tea at 5.30. Back in ward at 6 p.m. Put the remaining four children to bed, folding up counterpanes & changing day for night blankets, & taking temperatures. Did cyanide dressing on back of patient in 15 bed and combed the head of patient in 17 bed, a child who was scalded & whose head has been bandaged. Prepared & helped to give the 7.30 feeds to the children who are fed with bottle or spoon & made a fresh supply of Bengers Food. Changed my children's stone-cloths, put away the toys and filled a steam kettle for the child in 21 bed. Tidied the bathroom, it being set for operation. Gave my report to Sister & left the ward at 8.35.

MISS M.A. TOBIN

Entered Hospital March 26 1896

OCTOBER 17 1896, FEMALE SURGICAL WARD BEATRICE ♦ Today the ward is very heavy as we are well into our accident week. I am on day nurse's side of the ward so I first help to make beds. No. 1 is almost convalescent. Tetanus. Hers has been a most wonderful case. She has only been a few days in the big ward which she has very highly appreciated after three weeks solitude. No. 2 is an accident, very badly crushed fingers. 3 is one of our old chronic cases. She is a young girl with tubercular foot. No. 4 is a suppurating case that has now almost healed. 5 is a burn, but not very extensive or severe. In the next bed is a strangulated hernia. In 7 bed is rather a novel case. She is a little school girl whose chest was injured by a buss going over it. No. 8 is another tubercular foot, but she is quite an old granny. No. 9 is a little caries of spine. And altogether a very miserable little atom of humanity. 10 is an old rodent ulcer of the nose. It appears it was rapidly spreading & fast becoming malignant. At the operation one side of the nose was completely taken away & a graft put on. She is now in for a second grafting in some parts where it had not thoroughly taken. 10 [sic] is an old strangulated hernia rapidly becoming convalescent. 11 is a lupus of face. 12 is a very large woman who came in with a bad foot which rendered her thoroughly helpless. It has been found to be a perforating ulcer. 13 is rather an interesting case as they are not sure what is really wrong with her. It was thought she had a malignant growth & an abdominal exploration was performed which discovered nothing, but strange to say she got rapidly better after her operation. That was some five months since & she has come up again with all her old troubles returned. No. 14 is our second lupus. Her graft has taken very successfully & today she is very buoyant as her face is turned towards home. These are all my patients for this week as every bed is full. My time is fully occupied tending to their many and varied wants.

MISS E.M. HERITAGE

Entered Hospital October 1 1896

NOVEMBER 14 1896, FEMALE SURGICAL WARD ALEXANDRA ♦ This morning I entered Alexandra at 7 o'clock & being the third probationer I began my day's work by helping the night staff with the washings – The first to be done was a young girl of seventeen, who had been stabbed in the abdomen by a boy with

THE SEYMOUR WARD IN ST THOMAS'S HOSPITAL

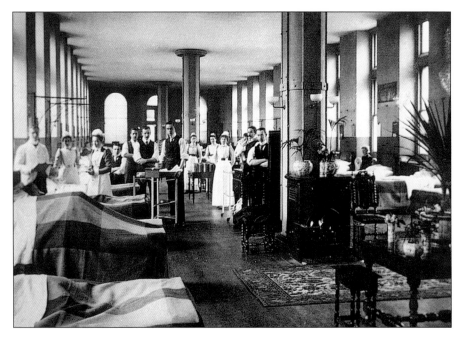

THE ALEXANDRA WARD. BEDS WERE ALWAYS ARRANGED IN NEAT ROWS DOWN EACH SIDE OF THE ROOM

a dinner knife. The weapon luckily did not pierce any vital parts & penetrated but a little distance thro' the abdominal wall. She is quite convalescent now & is returning home in a few days. My second washing I took to the bath as she was for operation in the afternoon. She was suffering from an acute disease of the Great Trochanter of many years standing. She has been operated on four or five times before, as she is constantly having large abscesses form in the hip. At 7.30 I went over to the day nurse's side. The first patient to be washed there was a dear little girl of five who had arthrectomy performed in her right knee some months ago at Guy's Hospital now the knee is swelling again considerably & the whole limb contracting, she wears a splint and an extension, besides this she has slight caries of the spine.

I next washed a little girl who had been operated upon for a tubercular gland on the left side of the neck. My next patient was one who had had nephrorrhaphy performed some five weeks back. The internal stitches caused suppuration, this was followed by a rigor on temperatures of 104°, accompanied by a septic rash covering the whole body. Now she is almost convalescent & allowed to sit up. During the time of her rash she was treated with antistreptoccocins given hypodermically into the abdomen, this caused a considerable drop in the temperature. I next washed a patient suffering from appendicitis, leeches have been applied to the spot over the vermiform appendix. She has had no great pain since her entry into the hospital. After prayers I took up my own work which consisted of washing sister's & the wine table, & the centre doctor's table & dusting every article upon these tables. Then there were the lunches to be given & the little nine months' old baby to be fed with bread & milk. He has had his knee opened & four tubes inserted for acute epiphysitis. After the mugs were cleared out there were the lamps to trim & refill, & the bath room to tidy & the slabs, basins & taps to clean & the mackintoshes to scrub. At 10.30 I went off duty.

MISS E.M.COOPER

Entered Hospital December 28 1896

FEBRUARY 10 1897, MALE MEDICAL WARD ARTHUR ♦ Got up at 6 a.m., dressed, breakfast, made my bed & dusted room by 7 o'clock & ready to go to my ward, "Arthur". Helped night nurse to make the beds on her side of the ward, 14 in number, rubbed the backs of patients, washed porringers & cleared away the urine bottles from the night before, dusted & polished window ledges all along my side & put in the thermometers for Sister. Prayers at 8 o'clock. About 8.45 went in the small ward to attend to patient there, who is very helpless, afflicted with spinal complaint. Washed him & dusted his room & tidied up there generally, afterwards tidied up the lavatory, washing basons, bottles etc. Off at 10.30. In time off, wrote out my lecture from notes taken at the class given by Home Sister on Monday morning last – on the "Alimentary Canal". Dinner at 12.45, on duty again at 1.30 p.m.

Went the round of beds, drawing sheets & making all tidy. Had a new patient to get to bed no. 15, came in with dropsy, he was bathed by bathman & I afterwards cut nails, combed his head & took his temperature which was 96°. Helped to make pads, of cotton wool & gauze. Visiting afternoon for the friends of patients. When they had gone, took teas in, did the 4 hour work; bottles round, assisted patients to get up, & put in the thermometers for Sister at 5 o'clock. Had some lovely flowers given me by No. 11, a man with bronchitis & umbilical hernia.

Off from 5–6 p.m. for tea-hour. Evening work. Took measurements of urine of 5; porringers & rubbed the backs, to prevent bed sores, with methylated spirit & cyanide ointment as required. Sponged small boy over with tepid water, who has acute pneumonia, his temperature being between 104° & 105°F. Washed window ledges & small tables & polished after with oil. Helped the probationer with all the beds, & settled off my side for the night, taking temperatures & making them all comfortable for the night.

List of patients' ailments on my side:

15 New patient suffering from Ascites & hydro-thorax, also umbilical hernia.
16 70 years of age, malignant jaundice, supposed cancerous growth in gall duct.
17 Old man – malignant growth in oesophagus, has great difficulty in eating.
18 Empty bed.
19 Boy in advanced stage of phthises.
20 Renal complaint – treatment hot air baths, injections of Pilocarpin & has been tapped.
21 Epileptic fits (patient going out soon).
22 Renal (Haematuria) blood in urine.
23 Acute Pneumonia.
24 Febright's Disease, been coming on for 10 years, youth lost the use of his limbs, & body much distorted.

25   Pleurisy with Effusion; aspirated twice since admission.

26   Bronchitis & Cardiac affection.

27   Abscess on liver, has much pain & difficulty in moving.

28   Renal disease & cirrhosis of the liver.

On my return to my ward at 1.30 I dusted the middle & washed the wine & medicine glasses and bathed a new patient suffering from a small lump in the right breast. After this I cleaned and refilled the glass jars containing tubes, catheters &c on the doctors' tables. Whilst finishing these I was called away to the theatre where one of our patients was having varicose veins removed from both legs. Mr Pitts was operating, assisted by Mr Fraser, his H.S. When this was finished I fetched the patient I had washed in the morning with hip disease. A large abscess was opened & six ounces of pus extracted. The femur was scraped & an india rubber tube inserted, & the wounds dressed with cyanide gauze spine wool. After my tea hour I washed the specimen glasses & test tubes that had been washed during the day & scrubbed all the theatre mackintoshes, aprons & then I dressed a patient who had been operated on for a mastoid abscess on the right side. She has a small tube through the ear which is syringed out with boracic lotion, and a boracic fomentation is applied.

After this there were the suppers to get, & the beds to be made with a fellow probationer – the middle to be tidied & the jugs & boiler to be filled, the night nurse's table to be prepared, the screen to be removed at 8 o'clock & the gases lowered and the bath room to be prepared for plaster, as an accident, Pott's fracture, had been brought in during the evening.

MISS M.L. CARTER

Entered Hospital January 28 1897

FEBRUARY 19 1897, FEMALE SURGICAL WARD ALEXANDRA ♦ When I came in the ward this morning I found that the night-nurse did not need me, so I started at once making beds. We had not got very far before the day-nurse sent me to begin my washings. I washed 2, 3 and 4. No. 2 is a dear old lady who has had a large lump removed from under her right arm, it is all bound up and she is quite helpless, but the stitches were taken out yesterday and she is going on very well. No. 3 is also old, but quite wonderful I think for she has just undergone her third operation & is doing splendidly, she had an abscess and her right breast was excised. I bathed her when she came in, & went down to the theatre with her, so though I am only third in the ward I feel very interested in those patients I can find out about. No. 4 is a little girl who had a tumour beneath her knee, she cries a good deal when it is dressed but otherwise is very good. Then I combed No. 9's head. She is a middle-aged woman who only came in yesterday afternoon & we had to get her ready for the theatre in a great hurry. She had a large abscess on her leg, but seems quite bright today & says she has very little pain now. The other operation case of yesterday, a girl who had a varicose vein removed, does not seem so well. I had finished before eight, so was early with my work this morning. I had finished nearly sister's table, the wine-table & the doctor's table by lunch-time & lunch was also early, as except for cutting thin bread and butter for 8 and 13, everyone had milk and bread. No. 8 has kidney disease, she has had one operation & is waiting for a second. No. 13 has been very ill, she had a tumour removed from her neck, & after that there was haemorrhage, so she had a special nurse for three days, but is better now. After lunch I did the lamps, glasses & tidied the bath-room, then as I was not wanted to help with any dressings, I carbolized porringers etc. and at 10.30 was off-duty. I went on again in the afternoon & tidied the middle, filling bottles for the doctors' table, then I sat down at the table with Sister & made bandages. It was visitors' afternoon & we had a great many flowers brought up, principally violets & snowdrops & a few daffodils. Then I bathed a new patient, who has kidney disease, helped to get the tea, & then it was time for my own tea. At six I washed & polished the hot pipes, got the middle all ready for night, removing flowers & putting lamps ready. Then I tidied the bath-room, & turned out a large cupboard where all the splints & extensions are kept. This was very untidy, & took me nearly till eight, when I washed up glasses, turned out gas & lighted lamps ready for the night. I had quite finished by eight & so had my fellow probationers, so we sat at the table & studied bed-tickets till 8.30 when Sister came, & after reports were given came Home.

Contemporary photographs of wards at St Thomas's show the neat arrangement of the beds down each side, at a standard distance apart, and the row of various tables down the middle of the room – Sister's table, the doctors' table, the spray table and the wine table (for medicinal brandy and the like). Ward routines ran like clockwork. These probationer nurses spent only one year at the training school before qualifying and moving on to other positions of responsibility within St Thomas's or at other hospitals.

NURSING STAFF AT ST THOMAS'S

THE NURSES' DINING ROOM AT ST THOMAS'S. TEA WAS SERVED FROM 5–6PM

THE REVEREND JAMES WOODROFFE

Curate

The Revd James Woodroffe was one of the curates at St Matthew's Church, Bethnal Green, in the poorest district of Victorian London – an area where, according to Charles Booth's famous social survey, 45 per cent of the population lived below subsistence level. The curate was Irish and had taken his degree at Trinity College, Dublin. Now he was dealing on a day-to-day basis with the social as well as the religious needs of a working-class slum parish. Woodroffe kept a working diary, not a personal one, though he permitted himself the odd pithy comment on those who called. His daily record gives a vivid impression of the urgent problems besetting his parishioners, who looked to the clergy for assistance at a time when the state safety net was a rudimentary one. An experienced priest with a limited range of help at his disposal (including referral to the Charity Organisation Society or to the Poor Law Guardians), James Woodroffe assessed each applicant with caution and, occasionally, a jaundiced eye.

AUGUST 23 1892 ♦ James Bailey, 8 Middle Walk, Blythe Street, late schoolkeeper of Abbey Street schools. Dismissed last January after many years' service in order to make a vacancy for a relation of one of the committee. At present he is Bell-ringer and Organ-blower at St Michael and All Angels (salary £8 per ann.). Comes about Parmiter Gift. Has received notice to quit after over 30 years' residence. A widower aged 64 years or thereabouts. His married daughter lives with him and brings in about 3/4d a week. Her husband took part in the Great Dock Strike & has learned by loss of employment that the world can do without him. He is in hope of being taken on at Tooley Street this week. The

August. -1892   2

of employment that the world can do without
him. He is in hope of being taken on at Tooley
St. this week. The problem is how is the old
man to live until the Parminter election. - Mr
Day has made application to the Brewery in
response to Mr Buxton's letter. - Told but Mr
Buxton & the manager are out of town. - Recommended Bailey to apply to C.O.S. & to lay his
case before the clergyman of S Michael's.

_____

Wednesday 24th   Wedding at 11 a.m.

_____

Widow Sarah Lyon - 5 Gilman St. Hackney
Rd accompanied by son a deaf mute who
has done no work for 16 weeks, wants assistance
from the Rector to whom she & her son
are known. - C.O.S. refused to help 6 weeks ago.
& the B.G. Guardians yesterday offered her
& her son the House. She declined as the
offer meant breaking up her home. Told her
the Rector was away, & I cd. not assist her.
She must now apply to the clergyman of
          her own district.
Mrs Susan Bickers 18 Paradise Row. re son Chas.
The lad is improving. - Sent him 3/ per Mrs
          Ockelford.

_____

Thursday 25th. Mrs Elizabeth Morris 66
          Abbey St. re A.D.L. for self
suffering from effects of confinement.
          Granted.
Mrs Elizabeth Bracken 24 Tyrrell St. re
A.D.L. for granddaughter Rebecca Tyler 29
Usk St. (aged 20 yrs) suffering from consumption

A PAGE FROM THE REVD WOODROFFE'S DIARY

problem is how is the old man to live until the Parmiter election. Mrs Day has made application to the brewery in response to Mr Buxton's letter, but Mr Buxton and the Manager are out of town. Recommended Bailey to apply to the Charity Organisation Society and lay his case before the clergyman of St Michael's.

AUGUST 24 ♦ Widow Sarah Lyon 5 Gilman St Hackney Rd, accompanied by her son a deaf mute who has done no work for 16 weeks wants assistance from the Rector to whom she and her son are known. C.O.S. refused to help 6 weeks ago, and the B.G. Guardians yesterday offered her & her son the House. She declined as the offer meant breaking up her home. Told her the Rector was away & I cd not assist her. She must now apply to the clergyman of her own district.

AUGUST 29 ♦ Widow Jane Agambar 11 Gibraltar Walk owes 5 weeks' rent at 4/- a week. Her landlady has asked for 10/- down. Mrs Agambar has fallen back owing to bad health. The London Hospital doctor recommended her to give up the machine for a little time and to work at the shop. She earns there only 12/- a week, so she is going to work at home again. She comes here to borrow 10/-, promising to pay it back by instalments. Told her we never lend money, & that if she liked she might apply at C.O.S.

SEPTEMBER 19 ♦ Joseph Abrahams, 23 Hare St, a middle-aged man with an indistinct articulation & not over-bright intellect, says his wife was married here about six weeks ago to a man named James Knight. Told him we had no such marriage on our books & that if he wanted to punish the wife for bigamy he must apply to the police. Wedding at 12.30 between Othello Green (aged 23) and Widow Sarah McNally (aged 41, looks over 50). She may be Green by name but her complexion is decidedly yellow. As venture no. 2 is a hairdresser he'll be competent to supply her with a wig in due time. Meanwhile she'll give him many a wigging. I do not admire this verdant bachelor's taste, but "every eye forms its own beauty".

SEPTEMBER 20 ♦ Mrs Eliza Brant, 10 Wood St, re convalescent letter for child Ethel Annie, aged 9 years, recovering from quinsy. Two children have been treated by the parish for fever and are now away for change of air at a convalescent Home at the expense of the parish. Woman is a scrubber in the Whitechapel Infirmary. Husband now follows the calling of a drunkard & "goes on dreadful" in the place he would call his home. Was a postman for 23 years & received much consideration from the officials. Before final dismissal they took away his stripes, reduced his wages, took away his uniform, gave him back all these things & at last were obliged to give him the sack. Referred to C.O.S. Woman appears respectable and healthy.

OCTOBER 12 ♦ Visited widow Elizabeth Jones 44 Busby St & found her in bed suffering from dyspepsia (her statement). She is a laundry woman, & has one daughter aged about 12 years. At once she said she was weak & faint for want of nourishment & that her child would have to return to work without a meal. She had pledged her things to pay the Doctor. The child is employed as a silk winder from 8 a.m. to 8 p.m. by Mrs Goodwin of Church Row. Where are the School Board authorities? Gave her an A.D.L. & for nourishment told her she must apply to the Parish of the C.O.S. Said she'd die before asking for parish relief, & that there was no use in applying to C.O.S. as they had refused to send her to a Convalescent Home last May. As she seemed ill & got excited I thought the simplest way of removing myself from the premises would be to give her 2/- pending inquiries. This morning I called at the C.O.S. Their reason for refusing the Convalescent letter was that on inquiry the woman was not found respectable enough for recommendation to any Home. Rector says Widow Jones is to be dropped.

OCTOBER 26 ♦ Widow Elizabeth Jones 44 Busby St re assistance in the shape of firing & food. Told me she thought the Church was intended to help the poor. Told her plainly that the result of my inquiries respecting her was unsatisfactory. She departed saying she was a hard-working woman & that my soft impeachment of her respectability was "false & that I knew it".

AUGUST 14 1893 ♦ I visited Mrs Haddon of 45 Church Row yesterday (Sunday). She is a lodger in Butcher's house & pays her rent regularly. From inquiries, I learned that the child is suffering from rickets & injured spine & requires nourishment. The mother wishes to get the child for a year or two into some institution. She gave very vague answers to my question as to how long her husband had been in the Madhouse. But Mr Butcher & his family assured me that the husband has been continuously there for the last four years, that the woman had a man about 36 years of age living with her for three months, that as a result of this intimacy the child in question was born; that the man (putative father) has skedaddled; that at present she is 'carrying on' with another man, and that before the birth of this child she had given birth to another bastard which had died in the Workhouse. Sister Rush has been making inquiries about Mrs Haddon who is a person between 28 and 30 years of age. She has 2 legitimate children, assuming of course that she was married to Haddon. The question of the diseased child's legitimacy could easily be

ST MATTHEW'S CHURCH, WHERE THE REVD JAMES WOODROFFE SERVED AS A CURATE

determined by communicating with the Asylum. Unless the man visited his wife within the last four years, this child aged between 16 and 18 months must have come into the world 'promiscuous-like'. Women who in the unavoidable absence of their lawful spouses go in for luxuries must put up with the consequences. A man visits Mrs Haddon every Friday evening & remains about 1 ½ hours. During the visit the children are turned into the streets to play. Butcher told me this on Sunday evening, 27 August.

Later, James Woodroffe notes that Mrs Haddon's child with rickets died in the workhouse on 2 June 1894, and that on May 14 she had had 'encore un enfant'.

NOVEMBER 14 1893 ♦ Robert Tollow, 10 Wood St re Victoria Pk. Letter for self (consumption). Occupation a waiter. Was obliged to resign yesterday due to ill-health. Referred him to C.O.S. but he won't apply as 10 months ago he was refused help when destitute & out of a situation. He said if I wished to know his history I must ask his parents, not him. I asked why he did not continue as a patient of Guy's Hospital. He said it was too far & preferred V. Park Hosp. NB I notice one peculiarity about these Tollows, viz when you help one, several other members come upon you. I am not too favourably disposed towards this specimen. A waiter ought not to shut up a clergyman by saying irritably "Listen, listen!" He went away quite mortified because he could not have what he wanted at once.

AUGUST 19 1895 ♦ Maggie Ward, a young spinster, 32 Ramsay St living with people named Attfield for last four years, had a bilious attack on Friday & Saturday & feels rather shaky. Told her I had no letters for such slight ailments & that Fox the chemist wd. put her right for a few pence.

SEPTEMBER 17 1895 ♦ Mrs Elizabeth Garrod 39 White St wants recommendation for Lon. Hosp. Maternity Certificate. Husband Henry a labourer (aged 40 years) who only has occasional work. Four children living out of 10 confinements. Has paid for 8 confinements. Helped by Lon. Hosp. on two occasions. One boy aged 16 years earns 8/- a week as an errand boy. Rent 14/- a week, reduced to 2/- by lodgers. Lived there 13 years. Wife aged 37 years used to do table trimming work. Not able to follow it now as it affected her eyes. Earns from 1/- to 4/- a week at washing. Application granted.

James Woodroffe left St Matthew's, Bethnal Green, in 1896. He moved to become a curate in the prosperous London parish of St Saviour, Fitzroy Square.

ANDREW TAIT

Schoolboy

Andrew Tait was about 15 when he decided, in the spring of 1893, to keep a diary. He had grown up in New Cross, South London, and was about to move with his parents to the rapidly expanding Essex town of Ilford, which was fast becoming a London suburb. Perhaps this great change in his life motivated him to write down his thoughts and activities as he left his old friends and made new ones at another school. He was an intelligent boy with many interests, not particularly sporty (unlike his brother Jim), but sociable enough, keen on puns and slang and amused by everything. This record of his last days at school and his first in the world of work, accompanied by his own illustrations, conveys a vivid sense of his personality and a whiff of the late-Victorian social world he inhabited.

APRIL 29 1893, SATURDAY ♦ At last it has been decided! The house we are to remove to is 34 Woodlands Road, Ilford, Essex. It has taken some trouble to settle on one & I am glad it's settled. I will here insert a few notes on house hunting.

House hunting

It is no good to go round to an estate office & ask where the estate toff is and calmly accept his word that the house is perfectly dry, etc. You will probably find that, on the first rainy day, the cistern is the driest part of the house. You may hear of a house with creepers & find on entering that the creepers are inside.

The Lark Philosophical Society, of which I have the honour to be captain, was wild with grief (or was it joy) on hearing of my departure & unanimously decided that, as we were going to move, the Society would have a "blow out". The "blow out" was to consist of a journey by steamboat to London Bridge to visit the Tower & a ride on the Electric Railway. We, that is Barret, Kipps, my brother & I (there were 2 other members who did not turn up though they said they would come) started from New Cross at ½ past 2. We reached Greenwich

PAGE
39

A·D MDCCCXCIV:
1893.

Golden Number XIV

Epact 23

Solar Cycle 27 1894

Roman Indication 7

Julian Period 6607 ?

Dominical Letter G

Hegira 1311–12

Anno Diarii (Date of be-ginning this diary) 247 (days)

WORK ON ECLIPSES

1893 CALENDAR

1894 DE JANUARY 1 1894

BOSH SCIENTIFIC CLUB

BUNKUM ASTRONOMIC SOCIETY

ECLIPSE OF THE CALENDAR

Except the last two I frankly confess I dont know in the slightest what these mean. They are put in for the benefit of the People who **do** know.

JAN 1st Monday

The bells were ringing the old year out, and the new year A m Popular Song 189?

grotesque initials No 1

They were, last night. I lay awake to hear them. When we came here first we were able to hear the Barking chimes quite clearly, but since Bedford Rd has been built, the houses seem to ⟶ intercept the sound and we have not heard them. However ♭ last night, they rang out loud and clear all over the Clements Wood Estate. This afternoon I thought I would go and see what Rainham was like. It is 7 miles from.

SKETCHES IN ANDREW'S DIARY, CELEBRATING NEW YEAR'S DAY 1893

A PADDLESTEAMER DOWNSTREAM FROM TOWER BRIDGE

TOWER BRIDGE IN THE 1890S

in time for the 3 o'clock steamer to the Old Swan
Pier. The fare was 3d each and well worth it
too (considering that I did not pay it, as Papa paid it
for us). Greenwich Hospital looks much better
from the river than from the shore. The Society sat
in the stern & enjoyed itself muchly (I did
anyhow). These sketches are only adaptations of 2
old houses we passed, namely the 'King & Queen' &
'The Angel'.

   A band, consisting of a Harp and Violin, played part
of the time & played pretty well too. Some of the
warehouses are very large & massive, the ones on the
Surrey side being by far the largest. The Tower Bridge is large & imposing. It
will be opened some time this year. The tiles of it are being tiled. It has cost a
thumping lot of money already, & I hear that even when it is completed it will
cost a lot more because of the insufficient approaches to it. We nearly ran down
a lighter just before getting to it. I was first on shore when our boat reached the
Old Swan and nearly got my toes scrunched in so doing by the gangplank. Went
under the arch & along Lower Thames St – reason why – it was the quickest
way. Kipps does not approve of the street, as it is principally paved with pieces
of fish & other similar things. So the Society adjourns to Eastcheap. On the way
to it we pass Barret's father's shop. His father is dead now, but his name is still
up & the business goes on as before. Voyaged safely to the Tower & walked
along the wharf. Saw Traitors' Gate & some men trying to put a gun on its
carriage in the moat, which is dry. Could not get into the Tower itself as it was
just closing, so went to St Paul's. On the way went through Paternoster Row to
see the Boys' Own Paper office. Shut. St Paul's is very big but I think not so
grand as it is cracked up to be. Don't care for architecture of that style. Like
Gothic better. Fine dome which I did not go up. Kipps admires this style of
thing muchly – Barret doesn't. Barret has no mind for antiquities. Saw remains
of fire in St Andrew's Hill, St Paul's Quire School, & street in which Papa's shop
is. Entered Electric Railway Station at 20 to 6. Went into a room, after paying
fare, to wait as I thought. Saw no signs of railway or train. Suddenly the room
begins to move! Barret explains that it is a lift. Room stops moving. We get out
on a platform & see a train in front waiting for us. We get in. Very peculiar
carriages. Guard shuts the door & only opens it at the stations. The windows
are only 6 inches high. The carriages are lighted by electric light & cushioned

luxuriously. A sliding panel in the door bears the name of the station the train stops at next, & is changed at each station. We got out at the terminus, Stockwell, & had another go at a lift. The whole journey on the Eastern Railway only cost 2d. The engines were very peculiar & the door was at the end of the compartment. Walked to Camberwell Green. Very long it seemed too, but it was only 1 ½ miles. Took the tram home. Said good bye to Kipps & promised to write. He promised to write too, and send me the minutes of the Society. Papa and Mama were out when I came home. They were at Ilford having a look at the house.

APRIL 30, SUNDAY ♦ This day I got my first pair of 'trucks' & a new style of tie and hat. Trucks are too long & don't like them at all. The packing is going on & all the books are packed. It is somewhat awkward to write in my diary (see picture). Did not go to church. It has not rained for 2 months with the exception of a few showers of a few minutes duration & we hope for fine weather to flit in.

May Day still brought some traditional customs.

MAY 1, MONDAY ♦ Yes it is May, at least it May be. It was washing day today. In the afternoon Grandmama went away in a cab to Clifton Rd. She is going to lodge there during the moving. I went to school in the morning. The school is Montague House School & is in the New Cross Road. It will be my last morning there. I am very sorry to leave as I like the school. I left my pencil box etc to Barret & my ruler to Stringer. Barret gave me his address and Kipps'. His is 331 New Cross Rd, Kipps' is 93 Lewisham High Rd. My parting address to my teacher was as follows: (500 lines left out for want of space) "Many thanks for all the bother and worry you have given me. I shall always think of you. Ta-ta. So long. Tuchyerlast." There were no jack in the greens, but 5 richly decorated coal carts passed the top of our street. In them were boys who cheered and shouted. This is one of the customs of today. Anyone who likes to ride in the carts is allowed to, if they can climb in. The carts are driven at a speed of about 20 miles the hour.

MAY 2, TUESDAY ♦ Tomorrow! Only one day more! My coins & stamps are packed so is most other things. We are going to take several plants out of our garden & they are put in a basket all ready.

MAY 3, WEDNESDAY ♦ Unfortunately my diary was not unpacked till Friday so I will not put so much in these days as they deserve. Besides, we are so busy at

BANK STATION OF THE CENTRAL LONDON RAILWAY, PART OF TODAY'S LONDON UNDERGROUND

A RETURN TICKET ON THE
CENTRAL LONDON RAILWAY

present that there is not much time for diary writing – but now to the events of Wednesday. Fortunately everything was ready & packed so that the removal men had nothing to do but put the things in the van. The van came at 7 a.m. & Mr Jackes the owner of it, a man with fiery red hair, came to hurry the men up & get in their way in general; owing to his great exertions the van & a cart at last started; they were crammed full and were, I thought, a very heavy load. However, they got to Ilford at 5 to 4. They left several things that we wanted taken, particularly 2s worth of timber for a summer house which could easily have been put in the van. When the van had gone we sat down on the stairs & had a banquet of bread & cheese in which we were assisted by our washerwoman. Soon after this we started for Ilford, Mrs Kimber (our washerwoman) with us. They are building a new station at Liverpool Street where we changed carriages. We reached Ilford as the clock struck 4 pm. We found the cart had just arrived & with the men & Mrs Branch's assistance everything was in the house by 7. Mrs Branch stopped all night with us.

MAY 4, THURSDAY ♦ We are now at last in our new house & I must admit that it is a very nice one. Our cat doesn't understand it at all & was very wild yesterday. Today it has disappeared & we can't find it anywhere. I am sorry, because it is such a clever cat & I like it. I went to Barking today. It is an old town and contains many old houses. However, it is badly built & 'slummy' in some parts.

MAY 6, SATURDAY ♦ A good many things are now in their places but we are far from being tidy yet. Our poor old cat, after being away all yesterday & the day before, turned up this morning. Its whiskers were gone & its fur was singed & it had been burned in several places. It must have taken refuge in a chimney in which a fire had been afterwards lighted ... However, I hope it will soon be itself again. All our pictures are up and Mama has ordered oilcloth for the hall. We have stained the dining room floor in oak & got curtains for the 2 bow windows. In the afternoon I went with my brother Jim to Wanstead Flats. They are an open space forming the lower portion of Epping Forest & dotted with bushes of various kinds, hawthorns predominating. Saw a signpost pointing the way to Little Ilford. I intend to go there soon because the road looks nice that way.

MAY 7, SUNDAY ♦ Mama, Papa, Jimmy & I went to church this evening. The minister preached on the subject of Ascension Day, why was it not kept as Christmas Day is. He is going to hold 2 services on that day. One is to be a children's service; I wonder if I shall go? I fancy I won't but I don't know quite. *[He didn't.]*

MAY 13, SATURDAY ♦ Having admired Wanstead Park we decided to go there today. On the way 2 boys asked us if we would like to join a cricket club they are getting up. We thought we would and are going to play on Monday next.

MAY 15, MONDAY ♦ It has not rained now for 10 weeks & everyone wants rain. The ground is like iron & hisses when water is poured on it, we often mistake clods of earth for bricks & bricks for earth. The cricket match that was proposed on Saturday came off this evening. However, as one of the boys had a football, we played that instead. One of the boys who invited us is called Ned & I like him the best of the lot. The other is called Bob. There is a boy called North who is an awful duffer, almost as bad as me. Today the new station is open for traffic. This is an important day in the history of Ilford.

MAY 16, TUESDAY ♦ Also an important day. Hitherto there has been no fishmongers in Ilford except a stall occasionally open for the sale of fried fish. But today a shop has been opened near the Broadway under a man named Handley.

After an extended holiday, Andrew's parents arranged for him to go to a new school.

JUNE 6 ♦ I am to go! The school is decided on & tomorrow night I am to go round & see it! I rather like it than otherwise, for 5 weeks of holiday begin to pall on a chap at last. None of our lot know this as I only knew of it at supper. A boy named Clements wanted me to go to his school, but this one isn't it. It is known to the master as Tyne Hall & to the chaps as Sharps. A chap at our Cricket Club named Freeman swears awful, & last night he was 'chucked out' by Ned whose other name is Bayliss. But this evening there was talk of a match to be played next Saturday and as Freeman plays well they have taken him back again. Freeman is also a swindler and a cheat.

JUNE 7, WEDNESDAY ♦ We hev [sic] bearded the Sharp in his Tyne Hall! He hath immense teeth, biggest I have ever seen. But now to business. When we got to what seemed to be the front of the edifice, we looked & saw a bell. It was broken, & so a boy told us to jingle the letter box. We did so, & soon after were in the presence of some enormous teeth with a man tacked on to them. He looked orful strict & we were glad to escape. When we had jingled the letterbox Giant Blunderbore's wife – I mean Mrs Sharp – came up and hid us in the oven – it was a small room anyhow, and about the size of an oven. Old G-Sharp soon came in & discovered us & only released on payment of a ransom – generally known as skoolfees, & we escaped.

THE SINKING OF THE H.M.S. VICTORIA, WITH A GREAT LOSS OF LIFE

Well things have been so dull that, as this diary is meant to be interesting, I have not given a description of them. The most important event has been the Royal Wedding on July 6th. We saw the illuminations. There was a great crowd & it is evident that England will not be a republic for several days yet. There was a fight in the House between some of the Irish members. The Victoria, a great ironclad, sank with great loss of life off Smyrna. And I have been nearly shot. It fell out thusly. I was voyaging to Dagenham & was almost hit by some men out rook shooting. Now we are going to Scotland, Saughtree [in Roxburghshire] is the name of the place, it is my Grandmother's farm & I expect to enjoy myself.

AUGUST 25 ♦ After tea grandma went to no. 29. She is going to lodge there while we go to Scotland. Papa is not going with us, he thinks the place where we are going is too dull & is going to Deal instead. Well the place is rather out of the way, being miles from Newcastleton, the nearest village. It has however a station of its own.

DECEMBER 21 1893 ♦ Shortest day! Yes, t'was the breaking up this morning. I got the first prize, by examination, while W. Searle (a boarder) the first by ordinary work. My villainous brother got the 1st prize for being the best boy in school. He is pretty good at school ... but at Home! Skwawks.

DECEMBER 22 ♦ Nothing of particular note this morning. Several messages "down the village" – this expression, common enough formerly, is now dying out rapidly as Ilford is no longer a village but a town of 15,000 inhabitants.

DECEMBER 25 ♦ I cannot put in anything about today though lots happened. Important days seem more difficult to describe than less important ones, to me. Therefore, except to say that I enjoyed myself muchly, I shall not write about today's doings.

JANUARY 1 1894, MONDAY ♦ "The bells were ringing the old year out and the new year in" – they were, last night. I lay awake to hear them. When we came here first we were able to hear the Barking chimes quite clearly, but since Bedford Road has been built the houses seem to intercept the sound and we have not heard them. However, last night they rang out loud and clear all over the Clements Wood Estate.

JANUARY 3 ♦ We saw a black and white cat sitting on our windowsill. It had been there all day so Mama took it in. Our old cat has been poisoned, so if no one claims this one, we'll keep it.

JANUARY 5 ♦ I went this evening to what the bills describe as The Winter Exhibition. The admission was a tanner & we lent a lot of curios to the African stall. The phonograph was by far the best I have ever heard; it recited (or phonographed) some words of Mr Gladstone, and so realistic was it, that it seemed as if the Grand Old Man was actually speaking to you in person, and had none of the metallic sound I have observed in the previous ones I have heard, and which is ludicrously like the dialogue of Punch & Judy. There was also a mummified cat, on which I quite expected to find a notice saying that this animal was fed on Thawley's Cat Condiment, but the notice only said that it was found in the Conservative Club when it was being done up this year. I can quite believe it. It was probably a stick-in-the-mud Conservative itself, who would rather be mummified than move on, or perhaps the result of the last General Election killed it.

FEBRUARY 11 ♦ I heard the first lark of the year this morning, & it 'hollered' several times during the afternoon. Poor lark! It will not have a tree to perch on soon. Bricks & mortar are smothering Ilford. Along the road to Cranbrook Park there were, a month ago, nothing but 2 large houses standing in wooded grounds. Now one of these is the estate office, of the 'Grange Estate', and where but a fortnight ago was a beautiful orchard is a hideous conglomeration of bricks & rubbish which are the primary ingredients for a road, while a noticeboard in another part informs the passer by that this is "the site of the Ilford Steam Bakery"! In Oaklands Rd, the next to ours at the back, several houses & a fire station are almost completed, while in the one immediately in front a large church is being built. Meanwhile a bogey in the shape of a Board School threatens the field in which we play football, just over our garden wall, and there is a rumour that Ilford College (the rival school to ours) and a row of houses is to be demolished and Roberts, the great draper, is to build one of his enormous shops on their site. Certainly we are getting on in Ilford, but in some things, I think, a bit too fast!

Andrew remembered that it was exactly a year since he started this diary.

APRIL 29, SUNDAY ♦ C'est moi, I'm still alive and kicking, I am still lazy, old-fashioned, mildly eccentric, artistic & unlike all other boys in general. Things are much the same – and different. My trucks are the same pair I wore this time last year! I intend to keep this diary up, if I can, & put what I like in it. As I have reminded the reader (for I suppose someone will read this sometime) this diary is written to please myself and folks who don't like must shut up. It's not their diary. Our estate owner, Cameron Corbett, MP has kindly given a whole

ANDREW'S DIARY IS FULL OF HUMOROUS SKETCHES

THE BARNARDO'S GIRLS' HOME IN ILFORD

URBANIZATION OF ILFORD HIGH ROAD

acre of ground which was no use to him as a recreation ground for the inhabitants if they choose to pay 5 bob a year. Paid, of course, in our case. It has only been opened a fortnight. Yesterday a 'garden party', so called, was held. So called, I say. My idea of a garden party is: best suit, do nothing but walk about, and everybody behaves as if they had got a bad attack of that disease called the 'snobs', dress suits and masher-appearance of everyone. Reality: a very enjoyable afternoon, songs, playing and recitations on a temporary platform. One of these was an imitation of village penny readings by Cobham. These were really capitally done. First came Tennyson's 'Queen of the May' as delivered by the village pastor in a deep bass voice. Next the squire gave 'Laidy Clawah Veah de Veah' in a very aristocratic voice but as he had lost the book and tried to recollect it from memory the effect was a failure. An 'Irishman' gave 'The charrg of the Loight Breegaid' and a 'dutchman' some other song I couldn't catch the title of. A gentleman with a lisp gave 'The Bellth' by E.A. Poe and another with a bad cold gave a love song in which the lines ending 'miss you' and 'kiss you' rhymed with others ending in a-atisshoo!! Everyone roared with laughter.

JUNE 17, SUNDAY ♦ Woke early and rose late as usual. I can't rise before Ma, and she is always late on a Sunday. Went to the bible class in the vestry of the Baptist Chapel. Subject: 'The woes of the drunkard' as it is called in the little blue paper which all members of the class are given ...

JUNE 20, WEDNESDAY ♦ As I write I can hear the strains of a steam organ which with a roundabout to which it belongs form the chief feature of a 'fair' which has settled on a field at the back of the 'Little Wonder' coffee tavern but which is fair in name only. It is frequented by the lowest class only and succeeds in making day, and a good proportion of night, hideous. Jamie, my brother, has been there. He likes such things in a way I cannot understand, but then neither can he comprehend my taste for antiquities and such like 'rot'. Jamie is, I am afraid, more 'like other boys' than I am. The 'new weather' which along with the 'new art, new humour' and other such fin de siècle humbugs has set in and everyone is heartily tired of it that I know of.

JUNE 21, THURSDAY ♦ 'A bootless errand'. This evening my boots are at the mending and I have only one pair, so I can't get out.

JUNE 23, SATURDAY ♦ This evening I went a walk to Chigwell. I passed by the Barnardo Homes mantled in many places with ivy and all a-twitter with birds and then came to the entrance. It was very pretty to me looking through the gate, what must it be to the waif from the grimy dens of Whitechapel? Today is the 2 anniversary of the founding of the homes.

JUNE 24, SUNDAY ♦ This is midsummer day – half the year is gone and half is still to come. I went to the bible class at the Baptist chapel and heard a very good address given by the Wesleyan minister and I have just returned from evening service at the Congregationalists. I intend to try and do more of the things that I should do and less of the things I shouldn't. Jim as usual did not go to church in the evening, he is always too tired to go.

JULY 7, SATURDAY ♦ Today I went nowhere except to the recreation ground where things important happened. Hewitt, a 'balmy' youth was ordered to clear off the green for certainly insufficient reasons. He refused and was ejected by the garden keeper, Mr Gay, somewhat roughly. But I and all the other boys brought him back in triumph and hooted the gardener. Fortunately just at the moment a thunder plump came on and the rebels rushed for a tent to take shelter in. They yelled and hooted and in spite of the efforts of Victor Banehr a big boy of 16, and myself, to restore order, they smashed the handles of three skipping ropes, wrenched the back off a seat, and made a large hole in the tent. At last we went home.

JULY 8, SUNDAY ♦ I went as usual to the class in the Baptist chapel in the afternoon and to the Congregational Chapel with Ma in the evening. After next Sunday the little iron chapel will give way to brick building next door which is still not nearly complete, no doors being in and the porch is also only half built.

JULY 9, MONDAY ♦ The Philosophical Conversation Club, a society started on the same lines as the old 'Lark', and all the members with one unimportant exception were present. We went down by the riverside in fields which were said to be private, but philosophers never care for these things, and as one of our rules is to resist all policemen, trespass boards & that sort of thing, of course we went. Mr Sharpe, our master, has taken a liking to me for some reason. About a month ago he asked me to go a walk with him to Greenstead Ch a short stroll of 30 miles and now he has lent me a local history as he knows I have antiquarian tastes. It is very kind of him and I appreciate it more probably than he thinks.

JULY 13, FRIDAY ♦ The grudge against Gay last Saturday having not been payed off, the wilder spirits, F. Shepherd at their head, thought this was a good time. I wasn't there, but I know what happened. F.S. had a mouth organ and started the performance with a symphony on it while the others shouted at the top of their voices songs of a mixed character. The row that followed simply baffles description. Hewitt yelled out 'Tarara-boomday', I don't care for Parnell or Gay', as Parnell is one of the principal men in the recreation society he didn't like that. The row was continued far past the closing time and Mr Gay was thrown several stones at. Then they winded all up by wrecking the tent and levelling it with the ground.

JULY 18, WEDNESDAY ♦ The conduct of the boys was the more caddish because the committee were thinking of getting up sports for them, and this evening Mr Henderson, the secretary, called us all into the pavilion from a game of Indians and said he wanted to say something about the sports but first he wanted to say something about the row last Friday. F. Shepherd was not present, nor Hewitt, but all the rest who took part in it were there & they had to write out a full apology and stand a severe jawing from old Henderson. We all think they were 'let off easy'. The last time I opened this diary I was a schoolboy. Now I am that no more. This afternoon I left school for ever. Everyone was happy at the end of term and opening of the summer holidays but among the shouting uproarious crew there was one who with difficulty suppressed the sadness he felt. Mr Sharpe shook hands with me and said he expected he would not lose sight of me altogether. He will not if I can help it. I suppose I should be very jolly now the summer holidays are here but I'm not. I'm very silly I know, but I can't help it. Everything seems to remind me that – I have left school. I expected yesterday that when our summer holidays were over I should have to go up to Mr Spicer's in Thames St, whom Pa has spoken to about me, about the beginning of September. So judge of my astonishment when this morning Ma told me that I was to go there before dinner today! Well we got here at length and Ma stopped outside while I went in, for Mr J. Spicer does not like parents coming with boys when they apply for situations because he finds the parents do all the talking. So I pushed open the swinging door and handed a note (from Pa) to an old man in a smoking cap who told me to wait a bit because Mr James was engaged at present. So I waited in the hall, meanwhile the queer old man in the smoking-cap said "how that man gets through his work I don't know" with other remarks not very complimentary to his employer. I gazed at the side of the hall with the row of stained glass windows & the little door behind which I knew the head of the firm was ensconced. I gazed at the clock and at the door as it swinged to and fro when people went out. I did this for at least half an hour and then the man in the smoking cap took in my letter on top of a great brown-paper package, into the office & soon after came out and told me I could go in now. I went through a large office into a smaller one with a window opening on

What d'you think has happened! The post office at New Cross, into which I have been scores of times, has BEEN BLOWN UP BY ANARCHISTS! Yes, all the front blown out and the place set on fire. Luckily no one was passing and the shop was shut for the night. The fire was put out and the letters saved with the exception of 4. The bomb was only in a cardboard case but for its size exceedingly destructive. Excitement reigns throughout New Cross. 400 anarchists are said to have arrived in England this week, and nothing can be done to prevent more coming. It is also said that as public buildings are so well guarded, the anarchists intend to have a num-ber of outrages on smaller buildings all over London. And yet these fiends are allowed to hold public meetings & hatch their devilish plots in peace. I hold it no murder but a commendable deed should one of these monsters be killed by anyone & I am sure the time will come when people will care more for their own

ANDREW'S ENTRY ON THE NEWS OF ANARCHISTS BLOWING UP THE NEW CROSS POST OFFICE

THE HIGH ROAD IN ILFORD

to the street. In a chair sat a tallish, pleasant looking gentleman who told me to sit down and then asked me whether I knew Latin, shorthand, arithmetic, what I did best, where I went to school, who was the master, where I lived, where Ilford was, when I left school (I answered 'yesterday afternoon, Sir' and he seemed amused). Then he called someone in and asked him where Mr Somebody was. He said he had gone out to dinner and so Mr Spicer gave me a piece of paper and told me to write my name and address. I did so. "Thanks, I think that will do" he said, wished me good morning and I went out. I think I made an impression on him, but of course nothing is certain.

AUGUST 6 ♦ This is my birthday. It is also Bank Holiday, so the road is crowded with brakes each with a bugler accompanied by his instrument of torture and generally using it to the best of his ability. I voyage with Pa to Hornchurch, a quaint old village with a fine Perp. church. We walked to Upminster. In the train going home we got into a carriage full of holidaymakers and as we passed Dagenham one of them said "Pretty, ain't it?" "Yus, but its a werry smorl plice". "But lookere, 'eres the 'ouses" said one of the others. "Oh well, any'ow they're only the dwarf v'ritee. Them sort o'houses is so small yer 'ave to reach darn the chimbley ter lock the door".

AUGUST 15, WEDNESDAY ♦ What d'you think has happened? The post office at New Cross, into which I have been scores of times, has been blown up by ANARCHISTS! Yes, all the front blown out and the place set on fire. Luckily no one was passing and the shop was shut for the night. The fire was put out and the letters saved with the exception of 4. The bomb was only in a cardboard case but for its size exceedingly destructive. Excitement reigns throughout New Cross. 400 anarchists are said to have arrived in England this week and nothing can be done to prevent more coming. It is also said that as public buildings are so well guarded, the anarchists intend to have a number of outrages on smaller buildings all over London. And yet these fiends are allowed to hold public meetings and hatch their devilish plots in peace.

AUGUST 16, THURSDAY ♦ The news of the outrage yesterday has spread, and everyone is talking of it. Although the statement that 400 of the anarchists had arrived is exaggerated, it is certain that 200 at least have arrived and have gone principally to Hammersmith, Stratford (which is only 3 ½ miles from here) and New Cross!

AUGUST 17, FRIDAY ♦ Tomorrow we leave for the seaside. Herne Bay is the watering place we have dignified with our patronage, and it is a nice place. I am in a mild state of excitement. I don't think I shall sleep much tonight.

AUGUST 18, SATURDAY ♦ I did sleep though, in spite of excitement and felt all right for the journey. We started off and reached Liverpool St where we got into a cab and drove to Holborn Viaduct. Our cabby managed to thread his way in and out very skilfully and by dodging up turnings when the road was blocked we got there in time. At last Faversham was reached. Our luggage was bundled out and into the Herne Bay train which was on the other side of the platform. Then after a stop at Whitstable we ran right into Herne Bay and we got out and bunked down for the beach while Pa and Ma managed luggage, lodgings etc. We saw a troupe of 5 'niggers', the 'HB Minstrels' who perform very well and have a wooden platform which they move from place to place. Then at last Pa came & told me it was time to go to the lodgings for they had got them at last. So we went to 58 Avenue Rd, a house kept by Mrs Clarkson. I am now there writing this and looking forward to a good time.

SEPTEMBER 4 ♦ The thing is decided, the die is cast, I am now a man of business, or I will be tomorrow, same thing. I yesterday received a postcard inscribed "Please favour us with a call when you are next this way" as if I went to the City every day. I went this morning to Spicers in response to the card & after being directed by the smoking-capped man, whose name I discovered is Marshall, I went to another man, the manager, who inquired if I was Mr Tait. I said I was & handed him the card. He asked me one or two questions & I answered them & he then said Mr Albert was engaged & I would have to wait. A troop of girls went into the stained glass windowed office and after that came out, went up and then down stairs with someone who was evidently Mr A. Spicer, then they went out. I waited altogether quite an hour. Then A.S. came back, held a confab with the manager, and then dosed me with a perfect volley of questions. Hearing I lived in Ilford he asked me if I knew the Banehrs! I was astonished, but answered pretty well. He asked me what church I went to, also if I had learned algebra, Latin, Greek, history and French, ignoring the 3 Rs & all the other subjects. Then he and the manager held another long confab & he at last went out. Then the manager told me to call here tomorrow at 9 & said that I would be taken on trial at 6 bob a week, & so I was appointed.

SEPTEMBER 5 ♦ At 50 Thames Street is James Spicer & Co's place of business and thither at 9 o'clock, or rather, before it, I wended my way. I saw the manager first of all, signed my name in the attendance book & was given some advice to the effect that I should get on as well as I possibly could, & then the manager showed me upstairs into a very large room at the end of which he stopped & gave me in charge of another man called Heslot, whose name is pronounced

TWO CLERKS AT THEIR HIGH DESK WITH TALL STOOLS

Haylot. This man with whom I was all day was rather glad to see me, as someone else in my department, called Wells, is off on his holidays and Haylot has been doing double work. I copied out of a tissue papered book called Letter Book into another called P.M. (why I don't know). Then I had to bunk all over the place which is of exceeding large size, with notes at different times. At 1 we bunked off for an hour for dinner which I took at the Arcadian (vegetarian) restaurant in Queen's Street. I did various things in the afternoon including putting the letters into the letter book. Which was done thus. The tissue paper pages were damped and then the letters laid face down, one on each page, or if they were ½ sheet size 2. A slip of yellow paper was put in on top of each page of letters. Then when the letters were used up, the book was put in a press which transferred part of the writing to the wet pages. Then the letters were taken out & the book is ready to have the invoices put into the P.M. book in the morning.

SEPTEMBER 6, THURSDAY ♦ Today my duties were varied by a visit to Dowgate Dock about some samples, but the ship containing them had gone to Millwall Dock. I also did checking off the items in the P.M. by entering the invoice items in a column by the margins. The principal difficulty I find is in trying to remember the names & desks of the many chaps in the office. I leave at half past 5 or 6 but don't have tea. The restaurant areas I pass going home give up very appetising smells of cooking & I have to content myself with these till I get home.

SEPTEMBER 13 ♦ One day here is very much like another. My duties are very numerous, too numerous to suit me quite, in fact. I attend to all the letters in evening, orders as well, for our dept. I book up all orders in the P.M. I attend to all our invoices. I take all Mr Beattie's notes for the various departments. Mr Beattie is Mr George's secretary I think, or something of that sort. I also am supposed to manage the railway advices, which I'm afraid I don't do, & look after all the stationery of our department. I also have to occasionally go out, and altogether I'm sure I do more than Wells, the man next to me. Mr Aylott has been away with a bad throat since Monday & as it's stocktaking time this is pretty rough on us.

Andrew is still not too old to enjoy Guy Fawkes' Day.

NOVEMBER 4, SUNDAY ♦ It is certainly a long time since I wrote in this diary. Things have changed but little, the principal difference is that I am now in the country department & attend to the packing notes. Royle, who previously had that post, is in my old place. The chap next to me is France, a very good-looking fellow, & not bad. Next to him is Clapham, who has pronounced socialistic views & is aged 19. Mr Keyzer is my manager now. Sometimes I have nothing to do at all, & again I may be up to my ears & over in work soon after. I have to take the packing notes for the warehousemen who are of course rather a rough lot. I am generally known among them, as 'Fireworks'. And this brings me to the great question of today or rather tomorrow. I intend to celebrate the festival of G. Fox [sic] in the usual manner whatever anyone says. I'm not too old to enjoy myself & so tomorrow,weather etc permitting, a grand display of 4 ½ d worth of firey workers will take place in the grounds of the Tait mansion at ½ past 7.

NOVEMBER 5 ♦ Heavy rain fell all day but cleared up sufficiently to allow the display to take place which it did. I did not get on well at business, but the jamboree compensated for that. Our guy, an Anarchist, burnt all right except the left leg which fell off.

Andrew's urge to explain everything fully led him to write another, undated page at the end of the volume.

I am still at Spicers, but the drudgery of the boards dept. is far behind. I got set down a peg or two after a month's muddling of the work, and have since risen till I am now Junior Clerk o' the Manchester Dept. under that same Wells aforementioned with Mr Cayser as manager. Aylott has left, Mr Marshall is dead & only the managers stick to the same posts as when I came. In Ilford our estate has almost reached its farthest boundaries. The Grange Estate is still larger, if anything, and the latest is that a great number of houses and shops on the north side of the High Street are doomed to instant demolition. Ilford College is now occupied as a Forest Gate Drapers Shop. The Board School has been built in Rutland Road.

Andrew Tait's business career continued until the First World War, when he became a driver in the Army Service Corps. After the war, he and his sister, who is not mentioned in the diary, moved to Birkenhead to look after their stepmother. Andrew became a sub-keeper at the Lady Lever Art Gallery and kept up his historical interests as a member of the Lancashire and Cheshire Historical Society. He died in 1969.

AUTHOR'S ACKNOWLEDGEMENTS

It has been a pleasure to collect the transcripts for this selection of diaries and to edit them for publication. Sincere thanks are due to the record offices and libraries listed below, to their staff for generous help and advice, and to the diaries' depositors. May I also record my gratitude to my colleagues at the Centre for Metropolitan History and the Institute of Historical Research for assistance and encouragement, and to my editors at Mitchell Beazley: Lynn Bryan (whose idea it was in the first place), Vivien Antwi and Michelle Bernard, for their cheerful and expert guidance.

BIBLIOGRAPHY

On Victorian Britain: Best, Geoffrey. *Mid-Victorian Britain*, 1851–75, Fontana, 1985; Briggs, Asa. *Victorian Things*, Batsford, 1988; Buck, Anne. *Victorian Costume and Costume Accessories*, Ruth Bean, 1984; Burn, W.L. *The Age of Equipoise*, Gregg, 1993; Christiansen, Rupert. *The Visitors: Culture Shock in Nineteenth-Century Britain*, Chatto, 2000; Emsley, Clive. *Crime and Society in England, 1750–1900* (2nd edn), Longman, 1996; Freeman, Sarah. *Mutton and Oysters: the Victorians and their Food*, Gollancz, 1989; Harrison, J.F.C. *Early Victorian Britain, 1832–51*, Fontana, 1988; Harrison, J.F.C. *Late Victorian Britain, 1870–1901*, Fontana, 1990; Hibbert, Christopher. *Queen Victoria in her Letters and Journals*, Sutton, 2000; Horn, Pamela. *The Rise and Fall of the Victorian Domestic Servant*, Sutton, 1990; Rubinstein, W.D. *Britain's Century: a Political and Social History, 1815–1905*, Arnold, 1998; Thompson, F.M.L. *The Rise of Respectable Society: a Social History of Victorian Britain*, Fontana, 1988; Wohl, A. S. *Endangered Lives: Public Health in Victorian Britain*, Methuen, 1984.
On Diaries: Batts, John Stuart. *British Manuscript Diaries of the Nineteenth Century: an Annotated Listing*, Centaur, 1976 ; Brett, Simon. *The Faber Book of Diaries*, Faber, 1987; Fothergill, R.A. *Private Chronicles: a Study of English Diaries*, OUP, 1974; Handley, C.S. *An Annotated Bibliography of Diaries Printed in English*, Hanover Press, 1997; Matthews, William. *British Diaries: an Annotated Bibliography of British Diaries Written between 1442 and 1942*, California U.P., 1950.

DIARIES' LOCATIONS

British Library, Department of Manuscripts: Joseph Hékékyan Bey (Add. Ms. 37456); Leonard Wyon (Add. Ms. 59617); and St Thomas's Hospital probationer nurses (Add. Ms 45814, Nightingale Papers vol. LXXVI); British Library, Oriental and India Office Collection: Maria Adelaide Cust (Mss. Eur.A.118); Cambridgeshire Record Office: George Pegler (854/F1, depositor Mrs Hill); Guildhall Library: Andrew Tait (Ms 10,383, depositor Mr J.F. Cooke); Hertfordshire Record Office: Arthur Peck (D/Ehx/B20); London Metropolitan Archives: Andrew and Agnes Donaldson (F/DON/29, Rear Admiral V. Donaldson) ; John Pritt Harley (O/54/1, depositor Dr J.B. Williamson); Amy Pearce (Rean papers Acc 2402, depositor Mr Stirling); and James Woodroffe (p72/MTW/140, deposited by the church of St Matthew, Bethnal Green); St Thomas's Hospital: Peter King (from their house journal *The Circle*, Sept. 1972).

CREDITS

Every effort has been made to contact copyright holders before publication, but this has not proved possible in all cases. The publisher will be glad to correct any omissions if notified. Maria Cust: copyright owner unknown; Agnes and Andrew Donaldson: Rear Admiral V. Donaldson; John Pritt Harley: copyright owner unknown; Joseph Hékékyan Bey: British Library Board; Peter King: Guy's and St Thomas's Trust; St Thomas's Hospital probationer nurses: British Library Board; Amy Pearce: copyright owner unknown; Arthur Peck: Hertfordshire Archives and Local Studies; George Pegler: Mr E. Hill; Andrew Tait: Mr J. F. Cook; the Revd James Woodroffe: St Matthew's Church; Leonard Wyon: British Library Board.

PICTURE CREDITS

Abbreviations: BL: British Library, BPL: Barnaby's Picture Library, GL: Guildhall Library, Corporation of London, HG: Hulton Getty Picture Collection, ILNPL: Illustrated London News Picture Library, LBR: London Borough of Redbridge Local Studies & Archive Collection, LMA: London Metropolitan Archive, MEPL: Mary Evans Picture Library, MOL: Museum of London.
Front Cover BPL/M. Buckland; 1 LMA; 2 top HG; 9 LMA; 11 top Cambridge Record Office; 11 bottom MEPL/J.L. Stewart; 14 top Cambridge Record Offices; 14 bottom Victoria & Albert Museum; 23 top BL; 23 bottom Royal Mint; 28 top MOL; 28 bottom HG; 35 top BL; 35 bottom BPL/F.A. Welti; 40 top MEPL/Institution of Civil Engineers; 40 bottom BPL; 47 ILNPL; 48 top GHL; 48 bottom HG; 53 Hertfordshire Archives and Local Studies; 59 top MEPL; 59 bottom MEPL; 62 Mansell/Time Pix/Katz; 67 BL; 68 BL; 73 top left LMA; 73 top right LMA; 73 bottom LMA; 76 HG/Colonel H W Verschoyle; 79 LMA; 81 top LMA; 81 bottom LMA; 87 Fratelli Alinari; 89 top right LMA; 93 centre LMA; 94 top LMA; 97 Fratelli Alinari; 101 BPL; 104 top LMA/*The Circle* magazine; 104 bottom LMA; 107 BL; 110 top LMA; 110 bottom LMA; 115 top LMA; 115 bottom Florence Nightingale Museum; 117 LMA; 120 Tower Hamlets Local History Library and Archive; 123 GHL; 124 top MOL; 124 bottom National Monuments Record/Crown Copyright; 125 top right GHL; 127 top BPL; 127 bottom MOL; 130 ILNPL; 133 GHL; 134 top Barnardo's Photo & Film Archive; 134 bottom LBR;138 top GHL; 138 bottom LBR 141 MEPL/Maurice Greiffenhagen.